LEED v4 BD&C
MOCK EXAM

Questions, Answers, and Explanations: A Must-Have for the LEED AP BD+C Exam, Green Building LEED Certification, and Sustainability

Gang Chen

ArchiteG®, Inc.
Irvine, California

LEED v4 BD&C MOCK EXAM :
Questions, Answers, and Explanations: A Must-Have for the LEED AP
BD+C Exam, Green Building LEED Certification, and Sustainability

Copyright © 2014   Gang Chen
Edition 4.0.3   Incorporated minor revisions on 12/30/14

Cover Photo © 2014 Gang Chen. All rights reserved.

Copy Editor: B.W.

All Rights Reserved.
No part of this book may be transmitted or reproduced by any means or in any
form, including electronic, graphic, or mechanical, without the express written
consent of the publisher or author, except in the case of brief quotations in a
review.

ArchiteG®, Inc.
http://www.ArchiteG.com
http://www.GreenExamEducation.com

ISBN: 978-1-61265-021-0

PRINTED IN THE UNITED STATES OF AMERICA

What others are saying about LEED BD&C Mock Guide ...
"A Valuable Book!
"The Green Building Certification Institute's LEED AP BD+C Exam have been developed to identify those professionals who have participated in the design and construction of energy efficient and environmentally sound buildings.

This book consists of two complete practice examinations that mimic the actual tests used. Then the correct answers to the questions are given and finally there is a short discussion on each question as to why the correct answer is correct.

This book should not be the first or the only book you use in preparation for the LEED AP BD+C Exam. First you should study the appropriate reference material, a list of which is given in the book. Then the sample exams can identify the areas in which you have trouble.

I recommend this book to everybody that wants to pass the LEED exam with no worries."
—AlexZ

"A Good Book!
"This is a very useful book. It provides general, entertaining, informative, educational and enlightening content about the LEED AP BD&C Exam and green Building LEED Certification. It not only has the LEED AP BD&C Mock Exam, but also has the answers and Explanations for the Mock

Exam. Some of the answers have the detailed calculations to make the answers more understandable..."
—**Tao Wang**

Dedication

To my parents, Zhuixian and Yugen,
my wife Xiaojie, and my daughters
Alice, Angela, Amy, and Athena.

Disclaimer

This book provides general information about the LEED AP BD+C Exam and green building LEED Certification. It is sold with the understanding that the publisher and author are not providing legal, accounting, or other professional services. If legal, accounting, and other professional services are required, seek the services of a competent professional firm.

It is not the purpose of this book to reprint the content of all other available texts on the subject. You are urged to read other available texts and tailor them to fit your needs.

Great effort has been made to make this book as complete and accurate as possible; however, nobody is perfect, and there may be typographical or other mistakes. You should use this book as a general guide and not as the ultimate source on this subject.

This book is intended to provide general, entertaining, informative, educational, and enlightening content. Neither the publisher nor the author shall be liable to anyone or any entity for any loss or damages, or alleged loss and damages, caused directly or indirectly by the content of this book.

USGBC and LEED are trademarks of the US

Green Building Council. The US Green Building Council is not affiliated with the publication of this book.

Table of Contents

Preface 13

LEED Exam Guides series by ArchiteG, Inc ... 21

**Strategies for Preparing for
LEED AP BD+C Exam 25**

**Chapter One LEED AP BD+C Mock Exam
(Including Both Part One and Part Two) 29**
- I. Important Note: Read this before you work on AP BD+C Mock Exam 30
- II. LEED AP BD+C Mock Exam 31

**Chapter Two LEED AP BD+C Mock Exam
Answers and Explanations (Including Both Part
One and Part Two) 101**
- I. Answers and Explanations for the LEED AP BD+C Mock Exam Part One 101
- II. Answers and Explanations for the LEED AP BD+C Mock Exam Part Two 129
- III. Where can I find the latest and official sample questions for the LEED AP BD+C Exam? 181
- IV. How was the LEED AP BD+C Mock Exam created? 181
- V. Latest trend for LEED Exams 182
- VI. LEED AP BD+C Exam registration 185

Chapter Three Frequently Asked Questions (FAQ) and Other Useful Resources...................187

I. I found the reference guide way too tedious. Can I only read your book and just refer to the USGBC reference guide (if one is available for the exam I am taking) when needed?............................187

II. Is one week really enough for me to prepare for the exam while I am working? 187

III. Would you say that if I buy your LEED exam guide series books, I could pass the exam using no other study materials? The books sold on the USGBC website run in the hundreds of dollars, so I would be quite happy if I could buy your book and just use that..188

IV. I am preparing for the LEED exam. Do I need to read the 2" thick reference guide? 190

V. For LEED V4, will the total number of points be more than 110 in total if a project gets all of the extra credits and all of the standard credits? 190

VI. For the exam, do I need to know the project phase in which a specific prerequisite/credit takes place? (i.e., pre-design, schematic design, etc.) 191

VII. Are you writing new versions of books for the new LEED exams? What new books are you writing?......................................192

VIII.	Important documents that you need to download for free, become familiar with and memorize	193
IX.	Important documents that you need to download for free, and become familiar with	194
X.	Do I need to take many practice questions to prepare for a LEED exam?	197

Appendixes **201**

I.	Default occupancy factors	201
II.	Official reference materials listed by the GBCI	202
III.	Important resources and further study materials you can download for free	206
IV.	Annotated bibliography	208
V.	Valuable web sites and links	209
VI.	Important Items Covered by the Second Edition of *Green Building and LEED Core Concepts Guide*	211

Back Page Promotion **217**

I.	*ARE Mock Exam series* (GreenExamEducation.com)	218
II.	LEED Exam Guides series	221
III.	Building Construction (ArchiteG.com)	231
IV.	Planting Design Illustrated	234

Index **238**

Preface

The USGBC released LEED v4 in GreenBuild International Conference and Expo in November, 2013. The GBCI started to include the new LEED v4 content for all LEED exams in June 2014. We have incorporated the new LEED v4 content in this book.

Starting on December 1, 2011, GBCI began to draw LEED AP BD+C Exam questions from the second edition of *Green Building and LEED Core Concepts Guide*. We have incorporated this latest information in our books. See Appendix 5 for Important Items Covered by the Second Edition of *Green Building and LEED Core Concepts Guide*.

There are two main purposes for this book: to help you pass the LEED AP BD+C (Building Design and Construction) Exam and to assist you with understanding the process of getting a building LEED certified.

The LEED AP BD+C Exam has two parts (or sections):

Part One is EXACTLY the same as the LEED Green Associate Exam. It has 100 multiple choice questions and must be finished within two hours (The total exam time for BOTH parts of the exam is four hours). In this book, "LEED AP BD+C Exam Part One," "LEED AP BD+C Exam Section One," and "LEED Green Associate Exam" are used interchangeably since they are EXACTLY the same.

Part Two is the LEED AP BD+C specialty exam. It focuses on information and knowledge related directly to green building design and construction (BD+C). It also contains 100 multiple choice questions and must be finished within two hours.

You can take Part One first, pass it, and gain a title of LEED Green Associate and then take Part Two in a different setting, or you can take both sections (Part One and Part Two) of the LEED AP BD+C Exam back-to-back in the same sitting. When a test taker fails one of the two parts, he can retake only the failed section of the exam at a later date.

The raw exam score is converted to a scaled score ranging from 125 to 200. The passing score is 170 or higher. You need to answer about 60 questions correctly for each section to pass. There is an optional 10-minute tutorial for computer testing before the exam and an optional 10-minute exit survey.

The LEED Green Associate Exam is the most important LEED exam for two reasons:

1. You have to pass it in order to get the title of LEED Green Associate.

2. It is also the required <u>Part One</u> (2 hours) of <u>ALL</u> LEED AP+ exams. You have to pass it plus Part Two (2 hours) of the specific LEED AP+ exam of your choice to get any LEED AP+ title unless you have passed the old LEED AP exam before June 30, 2009.

There are a few ways to prepare for the LEED AP BD+C Exam:

1. You can take USGBC courses or workshops. You should take USGBC classes at both the 100 (Awareness) and 200 (LEED Core Concepts and Strategies) level to successfully prepare for Part One of the exam. USGBC classes at 300 level (Green Building Design & Construction: The LEED Implementation Process) can be taken to prepare for Part Two of the exam. A one-day course normally costs $445 (as of publication) with an early registration discount, otherwise it is $495. You will also have to wait until the USGBC workshops or courses are offered in a city near you.

OR

2. Take USGBC online courses. Refer to the USGBC or GBCI websites for information. The USGBC online courses are less personal and still expensive.

OR
3. Read related books. Unfortunately, there are few official USGBC books on the LEED AP BD+C Exam, and, as of publication, no exam guides with sample questions. *LEED v4 BD&C Mock Exam* is one of the first books covering this subject and will fill in this blank to assist you with passing the exam.

To stay at the forefront of the LEED and green building movement and make my books more valuable to their readers, I sign up for USGBC courses and workshops myself. I review the USGBC and GBCI websites and many other sources to get as much information as possible on LEED. *LEED v4 BD&C Mock Exam & LEED v4 BD&C Exam Guide* are a result of this very comprehensive research. I have done the hard work so that you can save time preparing for the exam by reading this book.

Strategy 101 for the LEED AP BD+C Exam is that you must recognize that you have only a limited amount of time to prepare for the exam. So, you must concentrate your time and effort on the most important content of the LEED AP BD+C Exam.

LEED v4 BD&C Mock Exam provides you with a complete set of mock exams, including questions, answers, and explanations.

Most people already have some knowledge of LEED. I suggest that you use a highlighter when you read this book; you can highlight the content that you are not familiar with when you read the book for the first time. Try covering the answer and then read the question. If you come up with the correct answer before you read the book, you do not need to highlight the question and answer. If you cannot come up with the correct answer before you read the book, then highlight that question. This way, when you do your review later and read the book for the second time, you can focus on the portions that you are not familiar with and save yourself a lot of time. You can repeat this process with different colored highlighters until you are very familiar with the content of this book. Then, you will be ready to take the LEED AP BD+C Exam.

The key to passing the LEED AP BD+C Exam, or any other exam, is to know the scope of the exam, and not to read too many books. Select one or two really good books and focus on them. Actually <u>understand</u> the content and <u>memorize</u> it. For your convenience, I have underlined the fundamental information that I think is very important. You definitely need to memorize all the information that I have underlined. You should try to understand the content first, and then memorize the content of the book by reading it multiple times. This is a much better way than "mechanical" memory without understanding.

There is a part of the LEED AP BD+C Exam that you can control by reading study materials: the section regarding the number of points and credit process for the LEED building rating system.

Become very familiar with every major credit category and try to answer all questions related to this part correctly.

There is also a part of the exam that you may not be able to control. You may not have done actual LEED building certification, so there will be some questions that may require you to guess. This is the hardest part of the exam, but these questions should be only a small percentage of the test if you are well prepared. <u>Eliminate</u> the obvious wrong answers and then attempt an educated <u>guess</u>. There is no penalty for guessing. If you have no idea what the correct answer is and cannot eliminate any obvious wrong answer, then do not waste too much time on the question, just pick a guess answer. The key is, try to use the <u>same</u> guess answer for all of the questions that you are completely unsure of. For example, if you choose "a" as the guess answer, then be consistent and use "a" as the guess answer for all the questions that are completely unsure of. That way, you likely have a better chance of guessing more correct answers.

This is not an easy exam, but you should be able to pass it if you prepare well. If you <u>set your goal for a high score and study hard</u>, you will have a better chance of passing. If you set your goal for the minimum passing score of 170, you will probably end up scoring 169 and fail, and you will have to <u>retake</u> the exam again. That will be the last thing you want. Give yourself plenty of time and do not wait until the last minute to begin preparing for the exam.

I have met people who have spent 40 hours preparing and passed the exam, but I suggest that you give yourself <u>at least two to three weeks</u> of preparation time. On the night before the exam, look through the questions on the mock exam that you did not answer correctly and remember what the correct answers are. Read this book carefully, prepare well, relax and put yourself in the best physical, mental and psychological state on the day of the exam, and you will pass.

LEED Exam Guides series by ArchiteG, Inc.

Time and effort is the most valuable asset of a candidate. How to cherish and effectively use your limited time and effort is the key of passing any exam. That is why we publish the LEED Exam Guides series to help you to study and pass the LEED exams in the shortest time possible. We have done the hard work so that you can save time and money. We do not want to make you work harder than you have to.

Do not force yourself to memorize a lot of numbers. Read through the numbers a few times, and you should have a very good impression of them.

You need to make the judgment call: If you miss a few numbers, you can still pass the exam, but if you spend too much time drilling these numbers, you may miss out on the big pictures and fail the exam.

There are only a few official GBCI sample questions without explanations in the candidate handbook. The USGBC has been separated from GBCI and should have no clue of how GBCI constructs the LEED exam questions. Otherwise, the LEED exams will NOT be legally defensible. The existing practice questions or exams by others are either way too easy or way over-killed. They do NOT match the real LEED exams at all.

We have done very comprehensive research on the official GBCI guides, many related websites, reference materials, and other available LEED exam prep materials. We match our mock exams questions as close as possible to the GBCI samples and the real LEED exams. Some other readers had failed an LEED exam two or three times before, and they eventually passed the exam with our help.

Some authors rewrite the same information in a generic format for LEED Green Associate Exam, but I prefer to follow the LEED rating systems format that used by the USGBC for both exams and the related exam reference guides and not reinvent the wheel.

This will save you time because you know exactly what you have already studied after you have prepared for LEED Green Associate Exam, which is the same as part I of the LEED AP BD+C exam. You just need to spend maybe 30% more time (instead of double) to study for part II of the LEED AP BD+C exam (specialty exam).

After studying my books, you will become very familiar the LEED rating systems and you will be able to quickly locate the information in the USGBC reference guide when you work on the actual LEED projects. In fact, many of my readers simply use my book 90% of the time, and just use the USGBC reference guide to look up some very detailed information.

Other books on LEED Exams will become almost useless instantly once you pass the exam because they are NOT designed as a reference book, while my book, *LEED v4 BD&C Exam Guide*, is an exam guide AND a LEED reference book. It becomes even more valuable AFTER the exam.

All our guide books include study guide, a set of sample questions matching the real LEED exams, including number of questions, format, type of questions, etc. We also include detailed answers and explanations to our questions.

There is some extra information on LEED overviews and exam-taking tips in Chapter One. This is based on GBCI AND other valuable sources. This is a bonus feature we included in each book because we want our readers to be able to buy our LEED mock exam books together or individually. We want you to find all necessary LEED exam information and resources at one place and through our books.

All our books are available at
http://www.GreenExamEducation.com

Strategies for Preparing for
LEED AP BD+C Exam

There are several strategies for preparing for LEED AP BD+C Exam:

1. Bare bone strategy:
This strategy is bold, risky, but effective, low cost, and takes the least amount of time. You can spend about two weeks to prepare and pass the exam:

a. Download and read the latest candidate handbook for LEED AP BD+C Exam
b. Study the FREE PDF files listed at the end of the latest candidate handbook for LEED AP BD+C Exam (About 20% to 30% of the test content will come from these materials).
c. Study my books, *LEED v4 BD&C Exam Guide* and *LEED v4 BD&C Mock Exam* (Covers the fundamental and most important information of the remaining 70% to 80% of test content will come from these materials).
d. Do NOT buy or read the USGBC reference guide AT ALL

Pros:
a. Save time and money and still have a good chance of passing. In fact, a number of my readers did pass the exam using this approach.
b. You can prepare and pass the exam in about **two weeks**.

Cons:
a. Your score may not be as high as you want since you COMPLETELY skip the USGBC reference guide (probably range from 170 to 180).
b. You may feel nervous during the real exam. You may swear that you fail in the exam, and end up passing. You may have no clue why you pass but I know why you pass the exam though: my books cover the fundamental and most important information of the exam and set up a solid foundation for your LEED knowledge.

2. Middle of the road strategy:
This strategy is exactly the same as **bare bone strategy**, except that you do the following extra things:

a. Buy or read portion of the USGBC reference guide to supplement my two books:
Only refer to or read the USGBC reference guide for items you have questions, or for detailed information not covered by my books such as the "Behind the Intent" and "Step-by-Step Guidance" Sections and Calculations. I skip these sections in my book, *LEED v4 BD&C Exam Guide* because it takes too much time for you to read the information, and I think you should be able to handle most of the tasks covered in these sections if you MASTER the other sections.
b. Do a few extra sets of mock exams.

Pros:
a. Save time and money and still have an excellent chance of passing. In fact, many readers did pass the exam using this approach.
b. You can prepare and pass the exam in about **two to four weeks**.

Cons:
a. Your score may not be as high as you want (probably range from 170 to 185).
b. You may still feel nervous during the real exam.

3. Comprehensive strategy:
This strategy is exactly the same as **bare bone strategy**, except that you do the following extra things:

a. Buy or read the USGBC reference guide from cover to cover several times.
b. Write your own notes or create your own spread sheets based on the USGBC reference guide.
c. Do every set of mock exams that you can find.

Pros:
a. You have an excellent chance of passing if you can REALLY read the reference guide. In fact, several readers did pass the exam using this approach.

Cons:
a. Your score may be either very high or very low (probably either range from 180 to 200, OR fail).
b. You need to spend two months or more to

prepare and pass the exam.

c. You drag the exam prep process too long, and become tired of reading the USGBC reference guide, OR you can NOT find enough time to read the reference guide, and you end up failing the exam.

If you can pass the specialty exam, you should be able to pass the LEED Green Associate Exam. Make sure you download the PDF files listed in the candidate's handbook and peruse them.

All our books are available at **GreenExamEducation**.com

Check out FREE tips and info for all LEED Exams and ARE Exams at **GeeForum.com**, you can post jpeg files of your vignettes or your questions for other users' review and responses.

Chapter One
LEED AP BD+C Exam Mock Exam (Including Both Part One and Part Two)

Use the questions from the mock exam to prepare for the real exam. They will give you an idea of what the GBCI is looking for on the LEED AP BD+C Exam, and how the questions will be asked. If you can answer 80% of the sample questions correctly, you are ready to take the real exam. The 80% passing score is based on feedback from previous readers. You should read the study materials my other book, *LEED BD&C Exam Guide*, at least three times before you attempt the mock exam. Similar to the real exam, a question might ask you to pick one, two, or three correct answers out of four, or four correct answers out of five (some LEED exam questions have five choices). Generally speaking, if you do not know any of the correct answers, then you will probably get the overall answer wrong. You need to know the LEED system very well in order to answer correctly.

I have intentionally included some questions that you may not know the answers to. This is to help you practice making an educated guess.

I. Important Note: Read this before you work on LEED v4 BD&C MOCK EXAM

1. How much time should you spend on preparing for the LEED exam?

Answer: Some people spend too much time preparing for the LEED exam, and by the time they take the real test, they may have forgotten a lot of the information already.

Timing is VERY critical. If you pass the practice test with a score of 190 three months before the real test, by the time you take the test, you may have forgotten the information and score much lower.

One way to overcome this is NOT to take too much time to prepare for the LEED exam, and save at least one set of mock exam to use in the last week before the exam. You should NOT read any questions on this reserved mock exam until one or two weeks before the exam. This way, you can alert and energize yourself one more time right before the real exam, and work on your weaknesses. You can save the LEED v4 AP BD+C Mock Exam for this purpose.

There is one reader who passed the LEED Green Associate Exam or Part I of LEED AP BD+C

Exam by studying my other book, *LEED Green Associate Exam Guide,* for 10 hours in total.

For an average reader, I recommend not less than 2 weeks, but not MORE than 2 months of prep time. If you read my other book, *LEED BD&C Exam Guide*, you'll understand why too much prep time may hurt your chance of passing the exam.

II. LEED AP BD+C Mock Exam

Part One:
1. With regard to the credit, Optimize Energy Performance, who has the most influence in decision-making?
   a. MEP Engineer
   b. Architect
   c. Contractor
   d. Health Department Plan Checker

2. A project team should include the following as part of process energy: (Choose 3)
   a. Lighting that is part of the medical equipment
   b. Lighting included as part of the lighting power allowance
   c. Energy for water pumps
   d. HVAC
   e. Energy for elevators and escalators

3. A project team should include the following as part of regulated (non-process) energy:

(Choose 3)
a. Lighting for interiors
b. Refrigeration and kitchen cooking
c. Space heating
d. Service water heating
e. Energy for computers, office, and general miscellaneous equipment

4. With regard to LEED v4, which of the following LEED rating systems has fewer points for the WE category? (Choose 2)
a. LEED BDC NC
b. LEED BDC CS
c. LEED BDC Schools
d. LEED IDC CI
e. LEED OM EB

5. Which of the following are not considered laws?
a. USGBC LEED reference guides
b. Building codes
c. ADA
d. Municipal codes
e. EPA Codes of Federal Regulations

6. Which of the following buildings cannot obtain LEED certification? (Choose 2)
a. A new building that uses CFC
b. A new building that does not use CFC
c. A remodel project with a plan to phase out CFCs in 15 years
d. A building that uses natural refrigerants
e. A building that uses dry ice

7. Which of the following can reduce stormwater runoff and alleviate the urban heat island effect? (Choose 3)
   a. Increasing the site coverage ratio
   b. Increasing Floor Area Ratio (FAR)
   c. Using a vegetated roof
   d. Using porous pavement with high albedo
   e. Building a retention pond on the site

8. Recycled materials will contribute to which of the following?
   a. Traffic alleviation and smog reduction
   b. Protection of virgin materials
   c. Energy savings
   d. MEP cost savings

9. Which of the following is not graywater?
   a. Water from kitchen sinks
   b. Water from toilet
   c. Harvest rainwater
   d. Water from outdoor area drains
   e. None of above
   f. All of above

10. Which of the following is not blackwater? (Choose 2)
    a. Water from kitchen sinks
    b. Water from toilets
    c. Harvest rainwater
    d. Water from floor drains
    e. Rainwater that has come into contact with animal waste

11. Which of the following is not true? (Choose 2)
    a. Water from kitchen sinks can be reused for landscape irrigation or flushing toilets.
    b. Water from kitchen sinks cannot be reused for landscape irrigation or flushing toilets.
    c. Reclaimed water requires special piping with a different color.
    d. Reclaimed water cannot reduce potable water use.

12. Which of the following sets the baseline for water use? (Choose 2)
    a. Energy Policy Act (EPAct) of 1992
    b. Uniform Plumbing Code (UPC)
    c. WaterSense standards
    d. International Plumbing Code (IPC)

13. Which of the following sets the minimum standard of water use reduction?
    a. Energy Policy Act (EPAct) of 1992
    b. Uniform Plumbing Codes (UPC)
    c. WaterSense standards
    d. International Plumbing Code (IPC)

14. The State of California is building a visitor center on a 200,000 sf park. How big does the visitor center need to be, in order to meet the MPRs for LEED?
    a. 1,000 sf
    b. 2,000 sf
    c. 3,000 sf
    d. 4,000 sf
    e. There is not enough information to determine the minimum sf of the visitor center.

15. What is the maximum number of Regional Priority points a project can achieve?
    a. 3
    b. 4
    c. 5
    d. 6

16. The LEED O&M rating system is different from other LEED rating systems in which of the following ways:
    a. The LEED O&M rating system can be applied to any building type.
    b. The LEED O&M rating system emphasizes measuring and verification.
    c. The LEED O&M rating system emphasizes life cycle costing.
    d. The LEED O&M rating system deals with buildings after construction is completed.

17. Which program is used to qualify off-site green power for LEED?
    a. Green-e
    b. Center for Resource Solution
    c. Green Label
    d. Green Certified

18. Which of the following is the best to measure a material's ability to reflect sunshine?
    a. Albedo
    b. SRI
    c. Color
    d. Hue

19. Which of the following will not reduce materials sent to landfill? (Choose 2)
    a. Recycling
    b. Reusing materials
    c. Using regrounded materials
    d. Reducing materials used
    e. Reworking

20. Which of the following will not reduce materials sent to recycling facilities?
    a. Recycling
    b. Reusing materials
    c. Reducing materials used
    d. Reworking

21. Which of the following is the best statement regarding water savings for LEED credits?
    a. Water savings for LEED credits are per building codes.
    b. Water savings for LEED credits are per green building codes.
    c. Water savings for LEED credits are per federal regulations.
    d. Water savings for LEED credits are based on the percentage of water savings achieved by each design case as compared with a baseline building.

22. Which of the following is the best way to alleviate suburban sprawl?
    a. Build more low-rise, high-density housing.
    b. Provide underground parking spaces.
    c. Improve community connectivity.
    d. Provide more pedestrian walkways.

23. A developer has selected an urban site near a shopping center. This will help which of the following?
    a. Community connectivity
    b. Reducing urban runoff
    c. Community relationship
    d. Minimum city code requirements

24. Which of the following is considered open spaces for a LEED project?
    a. Landscape areas
    b. Tennis courts
    c. Sidewalks
    d. Areas under canopy
    e. Atriums with views to the ocean

25. A project seeking LEED certification may incur extra time for the following except:
    a. team member meetings.
    b. a city's plan check.
    c. commissioning.
    d. construction administration.

26. When should a project team start to plan a building's LEED certification?
    a. At schematic design
    b. At design development
    c. At pre-design stage
    d. At construction stage

27. For LEED certification, you should include the following as part of the project's area except:
    a. a parking lot.
    b. a landscape area.
    c. an interior space.
    d. a shared parking structure on an adjacent property.

28. A project team is working on a LEED BDC NC project. How much CFC-refrigerant can the team use?
    a. 2%
    b. 5%
    c. 7%
    d. None

29. Green-e is used for which of the following?
    a. On-site green energy
    b. On-site renewable energy
    c. Off-site renewable energy
    d. None of the above

30. Zero Emission Vehicles (ZEV) are defined by the standards set up by: (Choose 2)
    a. California Air Resources Board
    b. Center for Resource Solution
    c. ACEEE
    d. SCAQMD

31. You are working on a remodel project seeking LEED certification. What should you do about the existing HVAC units containing CFCs?
    a. Replace CFCs with dry ice.
    b. Replace CFCs with natural refrigerant.
    c. Replace CFCs with halons.
    d. Phase out CFCs in 10 years.

32. Which of the following is graywater?
    a. Water from bathroom sinks and kitchen sinks
    b. Water from bathtubs
    c. Water from toilets
    d. Rainwater collected in cisterns
    e. Stormwater that has not come in contract with toilet waste

33. For a building using a halon-based fire suppression system, which of the following is true? (Choose 2)
    a. Halons cause damage to the ozone layer.
    b. This building cannot seek LEED certification.
    c. This building must meet Fire Department requirements concerning halons.
    d. The halons must have a leakage rate of 10% or less.

34. What is the fundamental reason for global warming?
    a. Too many cars on the street
    b. The use of biofuel
    c. Too many green houses were built in the past century
    d. Too much Carbon dioxide
    e. Too much carbon monoxide

35. SMACNA address which of the following items related to LEED?
    a. Metal work
    b. VOCs
    c. Air quality during construction
    d. ODP
    e. Certified wood

36. For a project's initial research, what are some of the most important local issues? (Choose 3)
    a. Site orientation
    b. Parking regulations
    c. Incentives for sustainable design
    d. ACEEE
    e. TRCs

37. Which of the following statements are not true? (Choose 2)
    a. Bicycle racks will help community connectivity.
    b. High SRI pavement will alleviate the heat island effect.
    c. Green roofs can reduce stormwater runoff and alleviate the heat island effect.
    d. Retention ponds will not reduce stormwater runoff.

38. A construction waste management plan should include which of the following?
    a. The recycling capacity of the neighborhood recycle center
    b. Materials to be used for alternative daily

cover (ADC)
c. If the existing ceiling should be reused
d. The percentage of reused materials

39. A project team is seeking LEED certification for a building. The project can be certified under either the LEED BDC NC or LEED BDC CS rating system. How should the project team determine which LEED system to use? (Choose 2)
   a. Use the system that can gain most points for LEED.
   b. Ask the landlord for advice.
   c. Use the 40/60 rule.
   d. Make an independent decision.
   e. Use the 30/70 rule.

40. A project team is seeking LEED BDC NC certification for a building. Which of the following is true?
   a. The project team cannot seek precertification as a marketing tool for funding and attracting tenants.
   b. The project team can seek precertification as a marketing tool for funding and attracting tenants.
   c. The project must have a signed lease or LOI for at least 70% of the spaces.
   d. The project must be located in a new neighborhood.

41. A project team created a drive-by recycling program for the general public to recycle batteries and used electronics. The project team can gain a point under which of the following categories?
    a. SS
    b. MR
    c. IN
    d. EQ

42. What kinds of energy will generate the most pollution? (Choose 3)
    a. Wind
    b. Biofuel
    c. Gas
    d. Natural gas
    e. Nuclear power

43. Which of the following water saving items can be used for outdoor, indoor, and processed water? (Choose 2)
    a. Water efficient fixtures
    b. Sub-meters
    c. Native plants
    d. Water saving education programs

44. Which of the following analyze the potential savings over a building's life span?
    a. ROI
    b. Life-cycle analysis
    c. Life-cycle cost analysis
    d. Life-cycle saving analysis

45. Which of the following includes standards regarding major factors affecting human comfort?
    a. ASHRAE 55-2010
    b. ASHRAE 62.1-2010
    c. Green Label Plus
    d. Green Building Index

46. If you pass the LEED Green Associate Exam, what can you use on your business card?
    a. The GBCI logo
    b. The LEED GA logo per USGBC guidelines
    c. The LEED GA logo per GBCI guidelines
    d. The LEED Green Associate logo per GBCI guidelines
    e. The LEED GA designation only without any logo

47. A tenant purchased some furniture containing VOCs that was manufactured 450 miles from the job site. Which of the following LEED categories will be affected?
    a. SS
    b. EA
    c. MR
    d. EQ
    e. This project cannot seek LEED certification.

48. Green building through a holistic design approach will result in which of the following?
   a. Longer construction time
   b. Shorter construction time
   c. Extra cost
   d. Synergy
   e. Savings over a building's lifetime

49. A project team is seeking LEED certification for an 8-story building. The building has 8 equal floors, and the total square footage of the building is 168,000 sf. What is the building's footprint?
   a. 168,000 sf
   b. 42,000 sf
   c. 21,000 sf
   d. None of the above

50. For the same project mentioned in Question 49, if the total site area is 1 acre, what is the site coverage for this project?
   a. 48%
   b. 46%
   c. 43%
   d. 38%

51. For the same project mentioned in Question 49, if the total buildable site area is 1 acre, what is the FAR for this project?
   a. 438%
   b. 386%

c. 338%
d. 298%

52. A project team is working on a LEED project composed of 6 buildings on a campus. Each building is located on a 1 acre parcel of land. How should the project team determine the boundary of the LEED project?
    a. Each building should have its own LEED project boundary at the edge of the 1 acre land.
    b. The LEED project boundary should be the perimeter of the 6 acre site.
    c. The project team can make its own decision and determine the LEED project boundary.
    d. There is not enough information to determine the LEED project boundary.

53. A LEED project's landscape area includes which of the following?
    a. Green roofs
    b. Naturalistically designed retention ponds
    c. Sidewalks
    d. Vegetated roofs

54. Which of the following only applies to the LEED EQ category?
    a. ASHRAE Advanced Energy Design Guide for Retail Buildings 2010
    b. ASHRAE Standard 55-2010
    c. ASHRAE 62.1-2010
    d. ASHRAE/IESNA Standard 90.1-2010

55. Which of the following is considered a project soft cost?
    a. Carpet
    b. Doors
    c. Permit Fees
    d. Trees and shrubs

56. Where can a LEED Green Associate find the latest errata for LEED reference guides online?
    a. www.gbci.org
    b. www.nrdc.org
    c. www.usgbc.org
    d. www.epa.gov

57. The heat island effect can typically create ___ degrees Fahrenheit of change in temperature?
    a. 1
    b. 5
    c. 10
    d. 20

58. Who rules on CIRs?
    a. The Technical Advisory Group
    b. The LEED Administrator
    c. GBCI
    d. USGBC

59. Which of the following standards specifies minimum ventilation rates for IAQ Performance?
    a. ASHRAE 52.2-2007
    b. ASHRAE 62.1-2010

c. ASHRAE/IESNA Standard 90.1-2010
d. ASTM

60. Who of the following publishes GWP and ODP scores?
   a. The World Meteorological Organization
   b. ASTM
   c. USGBC
   d. The Global Climate Control Board

61. Which of the following are the most commonly used energy codes in the United States?
   a. Universal Energy Conservation Codes
   b. IPC by International Code Council
   c. International Energy Conservation Codes
   d. Energy Rating Codes

62. Which of the following is the most effective way to reduce stormwater runoff?
   a. Building a roof with high SRI value
   b. Using pavers with high albedo
   c. Grouping buildings together
   d. Adding trees to a parking lot

63. Which of the following sites is the best for community connectivity?
   a. A site close to the ocean
   b. A site close to a train station
   c. A brownfield site
   d. A site close to a shopping center

64. Choose the non-alternative-fuel vehicle from the following.
    a. A hybrid car
    b. A bus powered by natural gas with at least 20 mpg
    c. A fuel-efficient car powered by gas with at least 40 mpg
    d. An electric car

65. Which of the following is a car share membership program?
    a. Three or more people going to work in the same vehicle
    b. A program in which two or more people share the cost of a parking space
    c. A shuttle service program from a train station to work places
    d. A program for people to rent a vehicle on a daily or hourly basis

66. Which of the following must be certified under only one LEED rating system?
    a. 100% of the LEED project gross floor area
    b. 80% of the LEED project gross floor area
    c. Everything inside the property boundary
    d. 100% of the LEED project gross site area

67. Which of the following is graywater?
    a. Stormwater
    b. Laundry water

c. Dishwasher water
d. Water in retention ponds

68. Which of the following is used to measure a LEED building's environmental performance?
    a. Life cycle analysis
    b. Cradle-to-cradle analysis
    c. Whole building perspective
    d. Integrated design approach
    e. Overall energy reduction

69. If a LEED project has a CFC phase-out plan, which of the following must occur?
    a. The project can only allow 5% or less of annual CFC leakage.
    b. CFC must be replaced within 15 years.
    c. CFC must be replaced with CO_2.
    d. CFC must be replaced with halons.

70. Which two of the following have the same meaning? (Choose 2)
    a. Albedo
    b. SRI
    c. Refraction
    d. Reflection
    e. Solar Reflectance

71. What are RECs?
    a. The amount of fossil fuels avoided by buying renewable energy and expressed in kilograms
    b. The positive attributes of power generated by renewable sources

c. The amount of renewable energy purchased from a third party approved by the Green-e program
d. None of the above

72. The priorities for LEED projects are based on: (Choose 2)
a. Costs and benefits
b. Environmental guidelines
c. Carbon footprint
d. Project constraints

73. Construction waste reduction strategies include which of the following?
a. Purchasing materials manufactured locally
b. Using durable materials
c. Donating unused materials to charities
d. Burning the construction waste on site

74. Which of the following is the foundation of the LEED building rating system?
a. Prerequisites
b. MPRs
c. Prerequisites and credits
d. The triple bottom line

75. A project team is seeking LEED BDC NC certification for a 3-story residential building. Each floor is 600 sf. Which of the following is true?
a. The project team can seek LEED BDC NC certification because the building is

less than 100,000 sf.
b. The project team can seek LEED BDC NC certification because the building is more than 1,000 sf.
c. The project team cannot seek LEED BDC NC certification.
d. The project team can seek LEED BDC NC certification because it meets LEED's MPRs.

76. Per Montreal Protocol, HCFCs have to be phased out by:
   a. 1995
   b. 2010
   c. 2011
   d. 2030

77. If a building's wastewater overflows, which of the following can come into contact with potable water? (Choose 2)
   a. CO
   b. Toxic metal
   c. Grease
   d. Halons

78. The best way to prevent environmental impact caused by refrigerant leakage is to:
   a. Choose high quality plumbing materials, and perform high quality installation and maintenance.
   b. Use refrigerants without ODP.
   c. Design a building with natural ventilation and use no refrigerants.

d. None of the above

79. A project team is seeking LEED certification for a single building. What does the LEED project boundary include? (Choose 2)
    a. Only the portion of the site submitted by the project team for LEED certification
    b. Overlaps with the edge of the building
    c. Overlaps with the edge of the development
    d. The entire project scope of work

80. The economic benefits of green buildings include: (Choose 2)
    a. Reduced disturbance of wetland
    b. Lower water bills
    c. Increased use of rapidly renewable materials
    d. Better EQ and less liabilities

81. Which of the following is not a fossil fuel? (Choose 2)
    a. Gas
    b. Natural gas
    c. Biofuel
    d. Solar power

82. Which of the following needs to be implemented for water efficiency?
    a. A baseline of water use
    b. HET
    c. Waterless urinals
    d. Xeriscape

83. Which of the following is the most important feature of durability?
   a. The ability to endure and last for a long time
   b. Low maintenance
   c. Little or no unexpected extra costs
   d. Low maintenance and operation expense over the lifetime of the product

84. A project team is preparing a construction waste management plan. Which of the following should be included? (Choose 2)
   a. The removal of refrigerants containing ODP and GWP
   b. Recycle areas
   c. The removal and disposal of hazardous materials like PCBs
   d. The reduction of building size

85. For a LEED project, which of the following should not be used in a fire suppression system? (Choose 2)
   a. Dry ice
   b. Water
   c. HCFCs
   d. CFCs

86. Which of the following can earn points for Innovation? (Choose 2)
   a. Meeting the requirements of all LEED prerequisites and credits
   b. Exceptional performance above and

beyond the LEED requirements for an existing credit
c. Finding a solution responding to the project's regional priorities
d. Innovative performance in green building categories not covered by an existing LEED credit

87. A project team uses a strategy to earn an Innovation (IN) point for a project in California. Which of the following is true?
a. The same strategy can be used and guaranteed for an IN point in other projects.
b. The same strategy can be used for other projects in the same region.
c. The same strategy may or may not earn an IN point in another project.
d. None of the above

88. An office building uses ammonia (NH3) as a refrigerant. Which of the following is true?
a. NH3 has a higher ODP than HCFC.
b. NH3 has a lower GWP than HCFC.
c. NH3 is easier to leak out than HCFC.
d. CFC is easier to leak out than HCFC.

89. A project team is seeking extra points under the Innovation (IN) credit category. Which of the following is a feasible strategy? (Choose 2)
a. Set up a display area inside the building to educate the public on this building's

LEED performance.
   b. Try to gain more points than the original target level of LEED certification.
   c. Double the performance for a LEED credit.
   d. None of the above
   e. There is not enough information

90. Which of the following can be the most efficient way to save energy?
    a. Proper building orientation and fenestration
    b. High performance HVAC systems
    c. LEED certified equipment
    d. None of the above

91. Which of the following is not true?
    a. A LEED project team has to review the USGBC or GBCI website for previously submitted CIRs before submitting a new one.
    b. A LEED project team has to review the USGBC reference guide before submitting a CIR.
    c. All LEED rating systems can have CIRs except LEED ND.
    d. A fee has to be paid for each CIR submitted.

92. ASHRAE standards apply to all of the following except:
   a. SS
   b. WE
   c. EQ
   d. EA

93. Rainwater is:
   a. potable water.
   b. non-potable water.
   c. blackwater.
   d. raw water.
   e. graywater.

94. What are the most important criteria for a LEED building rating system?
   a. Quantifiable performances
   b. Prerequisites
   c. Credits
   d. Third party evaluations
   e. Third party standards

95. Which of the following cannot save water for landscape irrigation? (Choose 2)
   a. Mulches
   b. Perennials
   c. Hardscape
   d. Overhead irrigation
   e. Head to head coverage

96. Which of the following is true with regard to SSC: Heat Island Reduction? (Choose 2)
   a. Temperatures in urban areas can be 22°F

(12°C) higher than undeveloped areas and surrounding suburbs.
b. Urban heat islands contribute to 38.2% of regional warming according to a study of surface warming caused by rapid urbanization in east China.
c. The solar reflectance index (SRI) is used to measure the solar heat rejection of "non-roof" materials or components that are not considered roofing materials.
d. Measures to reduce heat islands measures include using a vegetated roof to insulate a building and extend the life of the roof or installing solar panels or shading devices.

97. Which of the following are most appropriate for a vegetated roof?
    a. Native plants
    b. Trees with large canopies
    c. Adaptive plants
    d. Lightweight plants
    e. There is not enough information to answer this question.

98. Which of the following is a prerequisite for purchasing green power? (Choose 3)
    a. The completion of the commissioning plan
    b. Communication with the key stakeholders
    c. Consultation with an electrical engineer
    d. Compilation of energy data

e. Evaluation of onsite and offsite energy choices

99. Which of the following is a pre-consumer recycled item?
   a. Aluminum storefront created from materials reclaimed from the manufacturing process
   b. Demolition concrete pieces used at another project
   c. Rigid insulation created from materials reclaimed from the manufacturing process of form cornice
   d. Scraps re-used in the carpet manufacturing process

100. A project team is seeking LEED Platinum certification for a school project. When can the project team advise the school board that the LEED Platinum certification has been achieved?
   a. After the project's substantial completion
   b. After the LEED registration is approved
   c. After the design review
   d. After the construction review
   e. After the LEED application is reviewed and approved by GBCI

Part Two:

101. With regard to submittals, what are the required documentation for Construction and Demolition Waste Management, Option 1? (Choose 3)
   a. MR Construction and Demolition Waste Management calculator or equivalent tool, tracking total and diverted waste amounts and material streams
   b. Total waste per area (if applicable)
   c. A list of manufacturers' names, product names, costs, and percentage of pre- and post-consumer content (if applicable)
   d. Documentation of waste-to-energy facilities adhering to relevant EN standards (if applicable)
   e. Documentation of recycling rates for commingled facilities (if applicable)
   f. Manufacturers' letters or cutsheets indicating the listed products' recycled content (if applicable)
   g. A plan showing the location of the recycle area

102. Building Life-Cycle Impact Reduction include the following options to achieve credits, EXCEPT:
   a. Historic Building Reuse
   b. Renovation of Abandoned or Blighted Building
   c. Building and Material Reuse
   d. Whole-Building Reuse

103. With regard to Minimum Indoor Air Quality Performance, the project team has the following options to obtain points? (Choose 2)
    a. ASHRAE Standard 170–2008
    b. ASHRAE 62.1–2010 or a local equivalent, whichever is more stringent.
    c. CEN Standards EN 15251–2007 and EN 13779–2007
    d. Chartered Institution of Building Services Engineers (CIBSE) Applications Manual AM10

104. For a LEED v4 BD+C: New Construction project with 200 parking spaces, including 6 handicap parking spaces (1 of them is van accessible), which of the following statements are true with regard to Green Vehicles? (Choose 2)
    a. The owner needs to designate 6 preferred parking spaces for green vehicles.
    b. The owner needs to designate 10 preferred parking spaces for fuel efficient and low emitting vehicles.
    c. The owner needs to provide electrical vehicle supply equipment (EVSE) a battery switching station
    d. The owner needs to provide electrical vehicle supply equipment (EVSE) or install liquid or gas alternative fuel fueling facilities or a battery switching station .

105. A developer is building a new retail building with 12,000 s.f. of gross leasable area. He intends to use 2000 s.f. as a leasing office and lease the remaining space to various shop tenants. Which LEED building rating system should he choose?
    a. LEED BD+C: New Construction
    b. LEED BD+C: Core and Shell
    c. LEED ND

    d. Either a or b
    e. None of the above

106. The US Army is building a 120,000 s.f. barrack, the building to site ratio is 1.5%. Which LEED building rating system should the project team choose?
    a. LEED NC
    b. LEED CS
    c. LEED ND
    d. This project cannot seek LEED certification.
    e. None of the above

107. For a LEED BD+C: Core and Shell project, which of the following statements is true?
    a. All LEED project team members have access to the CIR database and LEED Online after registration.
    b. The LEED project team may need to report post-occupancy water and energy use.
    c. The GBCI will inform the project team

credit is awarded or denied after design submittal.
d. None of the above

108. For a LEED for Homes project, which of the following statements is true?
    a. Homebuilders who intend to achieve LEED for Homes certification must contact a LEED for Homes provider organization.
    b. Homebuilders who intend to achieve LEED for Homes certification must contact a LEED Green Rater.
    c. A LEED AP carries out the thermal bypass inspection.
    d. None of the above

109. Which of the following statements regarding LEED are true? (Choose 3)
    a. CIR stands for Credit Interpretation Rulings.
    b. Precertification is for LEED BD+C: Core and Shell or LEED BD+C: New Construction.
    c. The USGBC will start to review your project 10 working days after receiving your submittal.
    d. A Green Rater is a professional who has shown qualifications for an energy rating certification, and demonstrates abilities to deal with a home's energy systems and performance.
    e. With regard to LEED Certification, you

have 20 days to appeal any comments from the USGBC. You need to pay $500 for each appeal.

110. Which of the following statements regarding CIRs are true? (Choose 2)
    a. If a LEED AP is not sure about where to place the handicap parking stalls, he can seek advice from the GBCI.
    b. One advantage of using a CIR is that it will let you know for sure if you can achieve a credit.
    c. Always review the GBCI and USGBC websites for previous CIRs before you submit one.
    d. If you cannot find a similar CIR, then submit a new CIR to GBCI online.

111. Which of the following statements regarding LTC: Reduced Parking Footprint are true? (Choose 2)
    a. Asphalt and concrete parking lots cover about 35% of the surface area in the average nonresidential areas.
    b. Parking is expensive, and costs developers and landowners about $15,000 per space on average in the United States.
    c. Locating projects in mixed-use, high-density areas or in places well served by transit can reduce parking demand.
    d. Preferred parking for carpools can increase parking demand.

112. Which of the following statements are not true? (Choose 2)
    a. The separation of the tasks for the USGBC and the GBCI is to meet the protocols of ASTM and ISO.
    b. To qualify for LEED BD+C: New Construction, a building must have a minimum area of 1,000 s.f.
    c. A portable classroom building may qualify for LEED NC or LEED Schools.
    d. A LEED project has to comply with environmental laws.

113. A fast food restaurant has leased a 950 s.f. space and is doing tenant improvement work for the entire space. Which of the following statements are true? (Choose 2)
    a. This project must meet ADA guidelines.
    b. This project can seek LEED BD+C: New Construction certification.
    c. This project can seek LEED ID+C: Commercial Interiors certification.
    d. This project cannot seek LEED certification because it is too small.

114. Which of the following statements are not true? (Choose 2)
    a. Green buildings employ an integrative approach and encourage the participation of key stake holders.
    b. A LEED project team may include facilities management staff, facilities O&M staff, community members, the

owner, and planning staff.
c. A LEED project team does not include product manufacturers.
d. A LEED project team does not include structural engineers.

115. What do you need to submit to achieve SS Prerequisite (SSP): Construction Activity Pollution Prevention for projects using local standards and codes? (Choose 3)
a. Drawings depicting erosion and sedimentation control measures implemented
b. A narrative detailing BMP and ESC and responsible parties.
c. Description of how project complies with local standards and codes
d. Field reports or shop drawing logs, product cut sheets, etc.
e. Comparison of local standards and codes with EPA CGP

116. SSP: Construction Activity Pollution Prevention may contribute to the following prerequisite or credits: (Choose 2)
a. SSC: Site Development—Protect or Restore Habitat
b. SSC: Heat Island Reduction
c. SSC: Open Space
d. SSC: Rainwater Management

117. SSC: Site Assessment may contribute to the following prerequisite or credits: (Choose 2)
    a. IPC: Integrative Process
    b. SSC: Light Pollution Reduction
    c. EAC: Green Power and Carbon Offsets
    d. EAC: Renewable Energy Production

118. A school district is building a 12,000 s.f., 2-story building on a previously graded 1-acre site. The building's first floor area is twice that of the second floor. To achieve SSC: Site Development—Protect or Restore Habitat, according to Option 1, On-Site Restoration, the project team needs to protect or restore at least how many s.f. of the site area?
    a. 8,000 s.f.
    b. 8,712 s.f.
    c. 13,068 s.f.
    d. 18,760 s.f.

119. A developer is doing a major remodel project. The LEED project team must exclude the existing MEP equipment in:
    a. MR Prerequisite (MRP): Storage and Collection of Recyclables, Option 3
    b. MRP: Construction and Demolition Waste Management Planning, Option 2
    c. MRC: Building Product Disclosure and Optimization—Sourcing of Raw Materials, Option 4
    d. MRC: Building Life-Cycle Impact Reduction, Option 1

120. To achieve point(s) for MRC: Construction and Demolition Waste Management, a project needs to:
   a. divert 50% and Three Material Streams
   b. divert 40% and Three Material Streams
   c. generate not more than 2.5 pounds of construction waste per square foot
   d. a or c
   e. b or c
   f. none of the above

121. Which of the following is related to most of the other credits?
   a. MRP: Construction and Demolition Waste Management Planning
   b. MRC: Building Life-Cycle Impact Reduction
   c. MRC: Design for Flexibility
   d. MRC: Construction and Demolition Waste Management

122. Which of the following statements are not true? (Choose 2)
   a. MRC: Rapidly Renewable Materials does not exist for LEED v4.
   b. Materials that are reused on-site are required to be repurposed.
   c. MR Credit Regional Materials. The 500-mile (805-km) radius requirement was decreased to 100 miles (160 km).
   d. Biobased materials are defined by the harvest cycle of the raw materials.

123. To meet EQP: Environmental Tobacco Smoke Control, a LEED project team needs to submit the following for Option 2: (Choose 2)
    a. Manufacturer's data sheets showing the air-tight properties of the partition.
    b. Any code or landlord restrictions that prevent establishment of no-smoking requirements.
    c. Test results for air quality in non-smoking areas.
    d. Door schedule demonstrating weather-stripping at exterior unit doors and doors leading from units to common hallways

124. Which of the following is NOT part of the minimum requirements for IP Prerequisite (IPP): Integrative Project Planning and Design?
    a. Owner's Project Requirements (OPR) Document
    b. Basis of Design (BOD)
    c. Preliminary Rating Goals
    d. Integrated Project Team
    e. Design Charrette

125. IP Prerequisite (IPP): Integrative Project Planning and Design applies to which of the following LEED BD+C rating system?
    a. Core and Shell
    b. Data Centers
    c. Healthcare
    d. Hospitality

e. New Construction
f. Retail
g. Schools
h. Warehouses and Distribution Centers

126. To achieve LTC: Access to Quality Transit, the project must meet the following requirements? (Choose 2)
    a. The project shall be located within 1/4 mile of walking distance of existing or planned bus, streetcar, or rideshare stops, or within 1/2 mile of one planned and funded, or one existing, bus rapid transit stops, light or heavy rail stations, commuter rail stations, or commuter ferry terminals.
    b. The project shall be located within 1/2 mile of walking distance of existing or planned bus, streetcar, or rideshare stops, or within 1/4 mile of one planned and funded, or one existing, bus rapid transit stops, light or heavy rail stations, commuter rail stations, or commuter ferry terminals.
    c. The transit service at those stops and stations in aggregate must meet a minimum number of trips.
    d. All distances above shall be measured from a main building entrance.

127. Which of the following statements is true with regard to LTC: Access to Quality Transit?
    a. A project team can achieve a maximum of 4 Points for LEED BD+C: Core and Shell Development
    b. A project team can achieve a maximum of 5 Points for LEED BD+C: Core and Shell Development
    c. A project team can achieve a maximum of 6 Points for LEED BD+C: Core and Shell Development
    d. None of the above

128. Which of the following statements are true with regard to Outdoor Water Use Reduction? (Choose 2)
    a. All projects using a LEED BD+C rating system MUST achieve Outdoor Water Use Reduction.
    b. Some projects using a LEED BD+C rating system do not need to achieve Outdoor Water Use Reduction.
    c. A project using a LEED BD+C rating system can achieve 5 points maximum through Outdoor Water Use Reduction.
    d. A project using a LEED BD+C rating system can achieve 2 points maximum through Outdoor Water Use Reduction.

129. Which of the following statements are true with regard to Water Metering? (Choose 2)
    a. All projects using a LEED BD+C rating

system MUST perform water metering.
b. Some projects using a LEED BD+C rating system do not need to perform water metering.
c. A project team can achieve points for water metering.
d. A project team cannot achieve points for water metering.

130. Which of the following statements are not true with regard to Cooling Tower Water Use? (Choose 2)
a. Cooling Tower Water Use is applicable for LEED BD+C: Healthcare projects only.
b. Cooling Tower Water Use is applicable for all LEED BD+C rating systems.
c. A project team can achieve a maximum of 2 Point for Cooling Tower Water Use
d. A project team can achieve a maximum of 3 Point for Cooling Tower Water Use

131. Which of the following statements are true with regard to EA Prerequisite (EAP): Fundamental Commissioning and Verification? (Choose 2)
a. The project team may need to finish the commissioning process activities for daylighting and lighting controls.
b. The project team may need to finish the commissioning process activities for mechanical and passive HVAC and refrigeration systems and related controls

c. The project team shall finish the commissioning process activities for wind, solar, or other renewable energy systems.
d. The project team shall finish the commissioning process activities for domestic hot water systems

132. Which of the following is not true regarding EQC: Low-Emitting Materials? (Choose 2)
    a. It is related to CARB.
    b. VOCs are from human-made materials only.
    c. This credit tackles each layer of the interior finish.
    d. Compared with VOC content limits, air concentration measurements from chamber testing predict emissions over time better, and can provide better protection for installers.

133. Which of the following is true with regard to LTC: Sensitive Land Protection? (Choose 2)
    a. It is related to LTC: Surrounding Density and Diverse Uses.
    b. A project tam can gain a maximum of 3 points for this credit, including 1 point for Exemplary Performance.
    c. Selecting a site that has previously been developed and limiting the building's footprint to the previously developed area is one strategy to lessen the environmental consequences of a

building.
d. Agricultural land conversion increases local opportunities to produce food.

134. Which of the following statements are not true with regard to EAC: Optimize Energy Performance? (Choose 2)
   a. A project team can only use the Prescriptive Compliance Method to achieve points for LEED BD+C: New Construction and LEED BD+C: Core and Shell.
   b. A project team can only use the Whole Building Energy Simulation Method to achieve points for LEED BD+C: New Construction and LEED BD+C: Core and Shell.
   c. A project team can achieve a maximum of 18 points for EAC: Optimize Energy Performance for LEED BD+C: New Construction.
   d. A project team can achieve a maximum of 20 points for EAC: Optimize Energy Performance for LEED BD+C: Health Care.

135. A project team is working on an office building, and the team wants to pursue LEED BD+C: New Construction certification under LEED v4. The team has reviewed the LEED NC scorecard and determined the maximum points the project can get are 55 points. What is the highest level of building LEED

certification they can achieve for this project?
a. Certified
b. Silver
c. Gold
d. Platinum

136. EAC: Renewable Energy Production Energy is typically handled at which of the following project phases?
a. Pre-Design
b. Schematic Design
c. Design Development
d. Construction Documents
e. Construction Administration
f. Occupation/Operation

137. EAC: Optimize Energy Performance is typically not handled at which of the following project phases? (Choose 3)
a. Design
b. Design Development
c. Construction
d. Construction Administration

138. A project team is working on a new building, and the team wants to pursue LEED BD+C: Core and Shell certification under LEED v4. Excluding In and RP, the team has reviewed the LEED NC scorecard and determined the maximum points the project can get are: 1 point for IP, 2 points for LT, 5 points for SS, 9 points for WE, 8 points for EA, 6 points for MR, 8 points for EQ. What is the highest

level of building LEED certification they can achieve for this project?
a. Certified
b. Silver
c. Gold
d. Platinum

139. With regard to EAC: Renewable Energy Production, which of the following may be Eligible Renewable Energy Systems? (Choose 2)
a. Wind energy systems
b. Geo-exchange systems
c. Architectural features
d. Geothermal heating systems

140. With regard to EAC: Renewable Energy Production, which of the following are definitely ineligible on-site systems? (Choose 2)
a. Wave and tidal systems
b. Biofuel-base electrical systems
c. Passive solar
d. Daylighting

141. With regard to EAC: Enhanced Refrigerant Management, which of the following are incorrect? (Choose 2)
a. A project may achieve 2 points for LEED BD+C: New Construction
b. A project may achieve 1 point for LEED BD+C: Core and Shell
c. A project may achieve 2 points for LEED

BD+C: Retail

d. A project may achieve 1 point LEED BD+C: Health Care

142. With regard to EAC: Enhanced Refrigerant Management, which of the following are correct? (Choose 2)
   a. Small water coolers, small HVAC units, standard refrigerators, and other cooling equipment containing less than 1.5 lbs. of refrigerant are not included as part of the base building system and are exempt from this credit's requirements.
   b. The credit is related to EAC: Optimize Energy Performance.
   c. Do not use fire suppression systems containing ozone-depleting substances like Halons, CFCs, and HCFCs.
   d. For more than one type of equipment, use a weighted average of all base building HVAC&R equipment based on cost.

143. With regard to SSC: Tenant Design and Construction Guidelines, which of the following are correct? (Choose 3)
   a. The project team may need to submit a guideline on tenant's energy use, including information on how to determine energy use and the related costs.
   b. The project team may not need an IPMVP-compliant M&V plan.
   c. The project team needs to show and

update the locations of any meters for measurement on a diagram.
d. The project team may not need to show and update the locations of any meters for measurement on a diagram.

144. Which of the following is used in SSC: Tenant Design and Construction Guidelines?
a. ASTM
b. ANSI
c. International Performance Measure and Verification Protocol (IPMVP)
d. ASHRAE

145. EAC: Green Power and Carbon Offsets is related to: (Choose 2)
a. Green-e Energy
b. Green Label Plus
c. Center for Resource Solution (CRS)
d. ASHRAE

146. Which of the following are incorrect? (Choose 2)
a. Paper, food, metals, glass, and plastics make up about 50% of the total municipal solid waste stream.
b. Based on percentage of weight, the remaining solid waste's ranking from highest to lowest is yard trimmings, textiles, leather, rubber and other, and wood.
c. The GBCI encourages you to compost food scraps and yard trimmings of waste

on-site if possible.
d. Yard trimmings cannot be composted on-site

147. Which of the following are true with regard to MRC: Building Product Disclosure and Optimization—Sourcing of Raw Materials? (Choose 2)
    a. Products sourced from manufacturers with self-declared reports are valued as one half of a product for credit achievement.
    b. Products sourced from manufacturers with self-declared reports are valued as one whole product for credit achievement.
    c. ASTM is part of the acceptable CSR frameworks
    d. ISO 26000: 2010 Guidance on Social Responsibility is part of the acceptable CSR frameworks

148. MRC: Design for Flexibility is related to the following credits: (Choose 2)
    a. MRC: Building Life-Cycle Impact Reduction
    b. MRP: Construction and Demolition Waste Management Planning
    c. MRC: Building Product Disclosure and Optimization—Environmental Product Declarations
    d. MRC: Furniture and Medical Furnishings

149. A project team can get one innovation point for MRC: Building Product Disclosure and Optimization—Material Ingredients by: (Choose 2)
   a. Purchasing at least 40 permanently installed building products that meet the credit criteria.
   b. Purchasing at least 50 permanently installed building products that meet the credit criteria.
   c. Purchasing at least 50%, by weight, of permanently installed building products that meet the credit criteria.
   d. Purchasing at least 50%, by cost, of permanently installed building products that meet the credit criteria.

150. MRC: Building Product Disclosure and Optimization—Material Ingredients is related to the following:
   a. ISO
   b. ASTM
   c. ASHRAE
   d. GreenScreen

151. Which of the following are incorrect? (Choose 2)
   a. A maximum of 6 points can be awarded for MRC: Building Life-Cycle Impact Reduction for LEED BD+C: Core and Shell.
   b. A maximum of 2 points can be awarded for MRC: Building Life-Cycle Impact

Reduction for LEED BD+C: Core and Shell.
c. A maximum of 6 points can be awarded for MRC: Building Product Disclosure and Optimization—Environmental Product Declarations for LEED BD+C: New Construction.
d. A maximum of 2 points can be awarded for MRC: Building Product Disclosure and Optimization—Environmental Product Declarations for LEED BD+C: New Construction

152. MRC: PBT Source Reduction—Lead, Cadmium, and Copper is typically handled at which of the following project phases?
a. Pre-Design
b. Schematic Design
c. Design Development
d. Construction Documents
e. Construction Administration
f. Occupation/Operation

153. Which of the followings are pre-consumer materials? (Choose 2)
a. Paper
b. Glass
c. Materials from regrind
d. Materials from rework

154. Which of the following must be included in the LEED submittal package for MRC: Building Product Disclosure and

Optimization—Sourcing of Raw Materials?
a. A list of actual materials costs
b. MR building product disclosure and optimization calculator or equivalent tracking tool
c. Corporate sustainability reports for 100% of products contributing toward credit
d. A list of manufacturers' names and manufacturers' letters or cutsheets
e. The percentage of recycled materials by volume

155. For a LEED BD+C: New Construction project, MRC: Building Product Disclosure and Optimization—Material Ingredients, Option 2, Material Ingredient Optimization is based on:
a. cost
b. weight
c. number of products
d. None of the above

156. A contractor is working on a LEED BD+C: New Construction project. How many points can he achieve for MRC: Furniture and Medical Furnishings?
a. 1 point
b. 2 points
c. There is not enough information to determine how many points he can achieve.
d. None of the above

157. For a LEED BD+C: New Construction project, how many points can a project team achieve for Construction and Demolition Waste Management Planning?
    a. 0 point
    b. 1 point
    c. 2 points
    d. 3 points
    e. There is not enough information to determine how many points he can achieve.
    f. None of the above

158. Which credit is related to EAC: Demand Response?
    a. EAP: Fundamental Commissioning and Verification
    b. EAP: Minimum Energy Performance
    c. EAC: Renewable Energy Production
    d. EAC: Green Power and Carbon Offsets

159. Which of the following project can choose EAP: Minimum Energy Performance, Option 3, Prescriptive Compliance: Advanced Buildings™ Core Performance™ Guide?
    a. Healthcare
    b. Laboratory
    c. Retail
    d. Warehouse

160. Which of the following is related to MRC: Building Product Disclosure and Optimization—Material Ingredients, Option

1, Material Ingredient Reporting? (Choose 3)
a. Chemical Abstract Service Registration Number (CASRN)
b. Health Product Declaration
c. Cradle to Cradle
d. EPA

161. MRC: Building Product Disclosure and Optimization—Material Ingredients, Option 3, Product Manufacturer Supply Chain Optimization, the document of the ingredients used to make the building product or building material is based on:
a. cost
b. volume
c. weight
d. None of the above

162. With regard to EQP: Minimum Indoor Air Quality Performance, a LEED project team must submit which of the following?
a. Confirmation that project meets minimum requirements of ASHRAE 62.1–2010, Sections 4–7
b. Controls drawing showing monitoring devices
c. Confirmation that project has MERV 11 or higher filters
d. Ventilation rate procedure

163. What is the Project Phase for EQP: Minimum Indoor Air Quality Performance?
a. Schematic Design

b. Design
c. Construction
d. None of the above

164. EQP: Environmental Tobacco Smoke Control is typically handled at which of the following project phases?
a. Pre-Design
b. Schematic Design
c. Design Development
d. Construction Documents
e. Construction Administration
f. Occupation/Operation

165. With regard to synergies, EQP: Environmental Tobacco Smoke Control is related to which of the following?
a. EQP: Minimum Indoor Air Quality Performance
b. EQC: Enhanced Indoor Air Quality Strategies
c. EQC: Indoor Air Quality Assessment
d. None of the above

166. Which of the following are not the responsible parties for IEQp3: Minimum Acoustical Performance? (Choose 2)
a. The Contractor
b. The Civil Engineer, Environmental Engineer, or Geotechnical Engineer
c. Mechanical Engineer
d. Architect

167. A LEED project team uses fly ash in concrete mixes. Which of the following statements are true? (Choose 2)
   a. The LEED project team may seek an Innovation Credit (INC) point because this is a reuse of pre-consumer content.
   b. The LEED project team cannot seek an INC point because this is already covered under an existing LEED credit.
   c. The LEED project team cannot seek an INC point because fly ash presents environmental challenges in reuse.
   d. The design team needs to get the owner's consent for using the fly ash.

168. EQC: Indoor Air Quality Assessment is related to which of the following Referenced Standards? (Choose 3)
   a. ANSI
   b. ASHRAE
   c. ASTM
   d. Carbon Trust
   e. ISO
   f. International Performance Measure and Verification Protocol (IPMVP)
   g. U.S. EPA

169. With regard to synergies, EQC: Construction Indoor Air Quality Management Plan is related to which of the following? (Choose 2)
   a. EAP: Minimum Energy Performance
   b. EQC: Low-Emitting Materials
   c. EQC: Indoor Air Quality Assessment

d. EAC: Enhanced Commissioning
e. EAC: Green Power and Carbon Offsets

170. With regard to EQC: Construction Indoor Air Quality Management Plan, which of the following are not true? (Choose 2)
    a. A project team can seek 1 point for this credit.
    b. A project team can seek 2 points for this credit.
    c. It does not apply to LEED BD+C: Core and Shell.
    d. It applies to LEED BD+C: Core and Shell.

171. A project team is working on a LEED NC project. Which of the following can qualify as a basic service for LTC: Surrounding Density and Diverse Uses? (Choose 3)
    a. A Chinese restaurant
    b. A law office with 20 employees
    c. An Olive Garden restaurant
    d. A public restroom
    e. A Ralph's Supermarket

172. What is the maximum number of points that you can earn for LEED BD+C: Core and Shell Development?
    a. 50 points
    a. 60 points
    b. 80 points
    c. 110 points

173. What are the different levels of LEED v4 BD+C: Schools Certification?
    a. LEED-SILVER, LEED-GOLD, and LEED-PLATINUM
    b. LEED-CERTIFIED, LEED-SILVER, LEED-GOLD, and LEED-PLATINUM
    c. LEED-BRONZE, LEED-SILVER, LEED-GOLD, and LEED-PLATINUM
    d. LEED-BRONZE, LEED-SILVER, and LEED-GOLD

174. How many credit categories are there for LEED v4 BD+C: New Construction? What are they?
    a. There are 4. They are Sustainable Site Development (SS), Energy and Atmosphere (EA), Indoor Environmental Quality (IEQ), and Regional Priority (RP).
    b. There are 6. They are Sustainable Site Development (SS), Water Efficiency (WE), Energy and Atmosphere (EA), Materials and Resource (MR), Indoor Environmental Quality (IEQ), and Regional Priority (RP).
    c. There are 7. They are Sustainable Site Development (SS), Water Efficiency (WE), Energy and Atmosphere (EA), Materials and Resource (MR), Indoor Environmental Quality (IEQ), Innovation and Design Process (ID), and Regional Priority (RP).
    d. There are 9. They are Integrative Process

(IP), Location and Transportation (LT), Sustainable Sites (SS), Water Efficiency (WE), Energy and Atmosphere (EA), Materials and Resources (MR), Indoor Environmental Quality (EQ), Innovation (IN), and Regional Priority (RP).

175. When did the USGBC release LEED v4?
    a. November, 2013
    b. April, 2014
    c. June 15, 2014
    d. June 23, 2014

176. Which of the following is not true regarding SSC: Rainwater Management?
    a. Conventional site development uses soil compaction.
    b. Low-impact development disrupt the natural water flow and water balance.
    c. The best way to manage rainwater is to pipe and convey runoff into large, centralized facilities at the base of drainage areas as quickly as possible.
    d. Green infrastructure (GI) rainwater management strategies and techniques mimic a site's natural hydrology, and improve upon the conventional approach. Project teams treat rainwater as a resource instead of a waste product.

177. Which of the following cannot be a High-Priority Site?
    a. A Historic District

b. A Federal Empowerment Zone site
c. A Brownfield
d. A flood basin
e. a, b, c & d
f. None of the above

178. Which of the following professionals is not involved in green building design?
a. Architect
b. Mechanical Engineer
c. Landscape Architect
d. Equipment Vendor

179. Which of the following are related to MRC: PBT Source Reduction—Mercury? (Choose 2)
a. MRC: Building Life-Cycle Impact Reduction
b. MRC: Building Product Disclosure and Optimization—Environmental Product Declarations
c. MRC: PBT Source Reduction—Lead, Cadmium, and Copper
d. MRC: Demolition Waste Management

180. For LEED v4 BD+C: New Construction, how many points are needed for Silver Certification?
a. 30 points
b. 40 points
c. 50 points
d. 60 points

181. For Construction Activity Pollution Prevention, ESC stands for:
    a. Environmental Safety Council
    b. Environment and Sedimentation Control
    c. Engineering Safety Council
    d. Erosion and Sedimentation Control

182. For LEED v4 BD+C: New Construction, Surrounding Density and Diverse Uses, you need to construct a building that:
    a. Meets density requirements within a ¼ mile radius AND has a certain number of diverse uses within a 1/2 mile radius of the site.
    b. Meets density requirements within a ¼ mile radius AND has a certain number of diverse uses within a 1/4 mile radius of the site.
    c. Meets density requirements within a ¼ mile walking distance AND has a certain number of diverse uses within a 1/2 mile walking distance of the site.
    d. Meets density requirements within a ¼ mile walking distance AND has a certain number of diverse uses within a 1/4 mile walking distance of the site.

183. To get point(s) for Access to Quality Transit, your building needs to be:
    a. Located within ½ mile of a subway or rail station that provides a minimum number of trips.
    b. Located within ¼ mile of two bus stops

that provide a minimum number of trips.
c. Located within ¼ mile of one or more bus stops for two or more bus lines that provide a minimum number of trips.
d. a and c.

184. You can get one point for Bicycle Facilities by locating the project such that: (Choose 2)
a. a functional entry or bicycle storage is within a 200-yard walking distance
b. a functional entry or bicycle storage is within a 150-yard walking distance
c. a functional entry or bicycle storage is within a 200-yard bicycling distance from a bicycle network that connects to at least one of the diverse uses
d. a functional entry or bicycle storage is within a 150-yard bicycling distance from a bicycle network that connects to at least one of the diverse uses

185. You can get three points for Optimize Energy Performance by:
a. Improving a new building's energy performance by 10%.
b. Improving an existing building's energy performance by 7%.
c. Improving a Core and Shell project's energy performance by 6%.
d. Both a and b.

186. Which of the following is not true with regard to EQC: Quality Views?

a. LEED BD+C: Health Care projects can get a maximum of 5 points for this credit
b. Up to 20% of the required area with access to quality views can now be into atriums.
c. View glazing in the contributing area can have frits.
d. 75% of all regularly occupied floor area must have at least two of the four qualified kinds of views

187. Which of the following are true with regard to EQC: Daylight? (Choose 2)
    a. Daylight reinforces circadian rhythms.
    b. This credit has advanced greatly and now focuses on using actual measurement and window design to approximate daylight levels and daylight quality.
    c. This credit is related to EAP: Minimum Energy Performance and EA Credit Optimize Energy Performance.
    d. This credit is related to SSC: Light Pollution Reduction

188. With regard to synergies, SSC: Open Space, is related to which of the following? (Choose 2)
    a. SSC: Heat Island Reduction
    b. SSC: Site Assessment
    b. WEC: Outdoor Water Use Reduction
    c. WEC: Water Metering

189. A project team is working on a LEED BD+C: New Construction project. The total site area is one acre, and the outdoor space is 15,000 s.f., including 8,000 s.f. of turf grass. With regard to SSC: Open Space, the project team can achieve
    a. 0 point.
    b. 1 point.
    c. 2 points.
    d. 3 points.

190. Which of the following is not true with regard to SSC: Places of Respite?
    a. Schools projects cannot achieve point for this credit.
    b. The area must be accessible from within the building or located within 200 feet (60 meters) of a building entrance or access point.
    c. The project team must provide additional dedicated places of respite for staff, equal to 2% of the net usable program area of the building.
    d. Options for shade or indirect sun must be provided, with at least one seating space per 300 square feet (27.8 square meters) of each respite area, with one wheelchair space per five seating spaces.

191. Chartered Institution of Building Service Engineers (CIBSE) is related to which of the following? (Choose 2)
    a. EAP: Minimum Energy Performance
    b. EAC: Enhanced Commissioning
    c. EQC: Interior Lighting
    d. EQC: Enhanced Indoor Air Quality Strategies

192. ASTM is not related to which of the following? (Choose 2)
    a. LTC: Reduced Parking Footprint
    b. LTC: Green Vehicles
    c. EQC: Low-Emitting Materials
    d. EQC: Thermal Comfort

193. Which of the following are true with regard to EQC: Thermal Comfort? (Choose 2)
    a. Thermal comfort is a complex amalgam of six primary factors including surface temperature, air temperature, air movement, humidity, metabolic rate, and clothing.
    b. Thermal comfort is a complex amalgam of five primary factors including surface temperature, air temperature, air movement, humidity, and metabolic rate.
    c. Predicted percentage of dissatisfied (PPD) and predicted mean vote (PMV) are two indices used as the referenced standards for this credit.
    d. Research administered by the

International Centre for Indoor Environment and Energy indicates allowing occupants +/–3°F of local temperature control can give rise to productivity gains of 2.7% to 7%.

194. Which of the following are not true with regard to SSC: Light Pollution Reduction? (Choose 2)
    a. When exposed to light pollution, some fauna and flora cannot adjust to seasonal variations.
    b. A project team must use backlight, uplight, and glare (BUG) rating method to achieve point(s) for this credit.
    c. Reducing uplight, glare, and light trespass can contribute to good lighting design.
    d. Illuminating Engineering Society and International Dark Sky Association (IES/IDA) Model Lighting Ordinance (MLO) User Guide and IES TM-15-11, Addendum A: ies.org is one of the two reference standards.

195. Advanced Buildings™ Core Performance™ Guide by New Buildings Institute is related to which of the following? (Choose 2)
    a. EAP: Minimum Energy Performance
    b. EAP: Fundamental Refrigerant Management
    c. EAC: Enhanced Commissioning
    d. EAC: Green Power and Carbon Offsets

196. ASHRAE 52.2-2007 is related to which of the following?
    a. EAP: Minimum Energy Performance
    b. EQC: Acoustic Performance
    c. EQC: Construction Indoor Air Quality Management Plan
    d. EQC: Thermal Comfort

197. ASHRAE Standard 55-2010 is related to which of the following?
    a. EAP: Minimum Energy Performance
    b. EQC: Acoustic Performance
    c. EQC: Construction Indoor Air Quality Management Plan
    d. EQC: Thermal Comfort

198. ASHRAE 62.1-2010 is related to which of the following? (Choose 3)
    a. EA EAP: Fundamental Commissioning and Verification
    b. EAP: Building-Level Energy Metering
    c. EQP: Minimum Indoor Air Quality Performance
    d. EQC: Acoustic Performance
    e. EQC: Interior Lighting

199. ASHRAE/IESNA Standard 90.1-2007 is related to which of the following? (Choose 2)
    a. EAP: Minimum Energy Performance
    b. EAC: Optimize Energy Performance
    c. EQP: Minimum Indoor Air Quality Performance
    d. EQC: Indoor Air Quality Assessment

200. ANSI is related to which of the following? (Choose 2)
   a. IPP: Integrative Project Planning and Design
   b. WEC: Outdoor Water Use Reduction
   c. WEC: Indoor Water Use Reduction
   d. EAP: Minimum Energy Performance

Chapter Two
LEED AP BD+C Exam Mock Exam Answers and Explanations (Including Both Part One and Part Two)

I. Answers and Explanations for the LEED AP BD+C Mock Exam Part One

If you answer 80 of the 100 questions correctly for a section, you have passed the mock exam for that section.

1. Answer: a
   The MEP Engineer has the most influence in energy performance, and the credit, Optimize Energy Performance.

2. Answer: a, c, and e
   The project team should include the following as part of **process energy**:
   Refrigeration and kitchen cooking, laundry (washing and drying), elevators and escalators, computers, office and general miscellaneous equipment, lighting not included in the lighting power allowance (such as lighting that is part of the medical

equipment), and other uses like water pumps, etc.

3. Answer: a, c, and d
   The project team should include the following as **regulated (non-process) energy**:
   HVAC, exhaust fans and hoods, lighting for interiors, surface parking, garage parking, building façade and grounds, space heating, and service water heating, etc.

4. Answer: a and b
   Points for the WE category:
   a. LEED BDC NC: 11 points
   b. LEED BDC CS: 11 points
   c. LEED BDC Schools: 12 points
   d. LEED IDC CI: 12 points
   e. LEED OM EB: 12 points

5. Answer: a
   Buildings codes, ADA, Municipal codes, and EPA Codes of Federal Regulations are laws, because they have gone through the legislation process, but reference guides by USGBC are NOT laws. They are rules set by the USGBC and have NO legal authority like the other governing agencies.

   LEED standards are voluntary. You choose to obey the rules when you seek certification for a building, but these rules are NOT laws.

6. Answer: a and c
   The manufacture of HVAC units containing CFCs was stopped in the United States in 1995. These units had been phased out from existing buildings located in the United States by 2011.

7. Answer: c, d, and e
   Increasing the site coverage or FAR will increase impervious area and will increase stormwater runoff. Porous pavement will help recharge the groundwater thereby reducing stormwater runoff, and high-albedo (high-reflectivity) materials will increase reflectivity to alleviate the urban "heat island" effect. Vegetated roofs and retention ponds can also reduce stormwater runoff and alleviate the urban "heat island" effect.

8. Answer: b
   Recycled materials can protect virgin materials, but may require more energy to process, can increase traffic, and increase MEP cost.

9. Answer: f
   Graywater is the household water that has not come into contact with the kitchen sink or toilet waste.

See USGBC Definitions at the following link:

https://www.usgbc.org/ShowFile.aspx?DocumentID=5744

The definitions on the PDF file that you can download from the link above should be read at least three times. Become very familiar with them and MEMORIZE. LEED exams always test these definitions.

10. Answer: c and d
    Blackwater, otherwise known as **brown water**, foul water, or sewage, is water from the kitchen sink, dishwasher, or water that has come into contact with human or animal waste.

11. Answer: a and d
    Read the question carefully; it is asking for the WRONG statements.

12. Answer: b and d
    Both the Uniform Plumbing Code (**UPC**) and International Plumbing Code (**IPC**) set standards for plumbing fixture water use, and their requirements for the water use baseline are the same in many cases.

13. Answer: a
    This question tests your knowledge of the Energy Policy Act (EPAct) of 1992.

Although called the <u>Energy</u> Policy Act, it deals with <u>water</u> savings. This is the trick.

14. Answer: d
MPRs include some very basic requirements. For example:
1) The building must be <u>1,000 sf</u> minimum for LEED BDC NC, LEED BDC Schools, LEED BDC CS, and LEED EB: O&M. There is a <u>250 sf</u> minimum for LEED IDC CI.
2) The building to site ratio must be <u>2%</u> or higher. 2% x 200,000 sf = 4,000 sf

15. Answer: b
The maximum number of Regional Priority points a project can achieve is 4 out of the 6 <u>possible</u> points. A project team needs to select which 4 of the 6 points to use.

16. Answer: d
The LEED O&M rating system deals with buildings after construction is completed. All other answers are not unique to LEED O&M.

17. Answer: a
You should use the definition of a renewable source given by the Center for Resource Solution's (CRS) in their Green-e product requirements to determine which power to purchase. The question is asking for a program, not an organization. Center for Resource Solution's (CRS) is an

organization, while <u>Green-e</u> is a program.

18. Answer: b

    Both albedo and SRI are good indexes, but SRI is the better option. SRI stands for Solar Reflectance Index.

19. Answer: c and e

    Pay attention to the word "not" in the question.

20. Answer: a

    When you recycle, materials are sent to recycling facilities.

21. Answer: d

    LEED is a system set up by USGBC, and not by the federal government or International Code Council (ICC). USGBC is NOT a government agency. Building codes and green building codes are set up by the local government per the ICC model codes.

    For LEED, water savings are based on the percentage of water saved by the design case when compared with a baseline building.

22. Answer: c

    Community connectivity is the best answer. The other answers have some merit, but they are not the <u>best</u> answer.

23. Answer: a
Community connectivity is the best answer. All other answers are distracters to confuse you. If you have a firm knowledge of community connectivity, you should be able to answer this question correctly.

24. Answer: a
Open spaces need to be vegetated and pervious areas. Areas under canopy and atriums with views to the ocean are typically not considered open spaces for a LEED project.

25. Answer: b
Pay attention to the word "except" in the question. LEED certification does NOT involve extra time or effort for a city's plan check or permitting.

26. Answer: c
For planning a project's LEED certification, the earlier this is done in the process, the better.

27. Answer: d
You cannot include a shared parking structure on an adjacent property as part of the project area, because it belongs to someone other than your project owner.

28. Answer: d
You cannot use CFC-refrigerant in new

buildings. LEED NC is a rating system for new buildings.

29. Answer: c

    <u>Green-e</u> product requirements written by the Center for Resource Solutions are used as guidelines for purchasing your building's electricity from <u>off-site</u> renewable sources. The purchase is based on quantity, NOT the cost, and contracts for this renewable energy should be at least <u>five years</u> long.

30. Answer: a and c

    Only vehicles classified as **Zero Emission Vehicles (ZEV)** by California Air Resources Board or vehicles with a green score of at least <u>45</u> on the **American Council for an Energy Efficient Economy (ACEEE)** annual vehicle rating guide are qualified as fuel efficient and low emitting vehicles for LEED credit.

31. Answer: b

    The manufacture of HVAC units containing CFCs was stopped in the United States in 1995. These units had been phased out from existing U.S. buildings by 2011. Halons are used for fire suppression systems, NOT HVAC systems. Dry ice is commonly used to preserve food, instead of being used as HVAC refrigerant.

32. Answer: b
Per UPC, **graywater** is the household water that has not come into contact with the kitchen sink or toilet waste.

33. Answer: a and c
Halons cause damage to the ozone layer, but a building using a halon-based fire suppression system can still seek LEED certification. This building must meet Fire Department requirements concerning halons.

34. Answer: d
Answers "a" and "b" have some merit, but they are not the fundamental cause of global warming. The rest of the answers are simply distracters.

35. Answer: c
The Sheet Metal and Air Conditioning National Contractors Association (SMACNA) has an IAQ Guideline for Occupied Buildings Under Construction.

36. Answer: a, b, and c
American Council for an Energy Efficient Economy (ACEEE) and Tradable Renewable Certificates (TRCs) are universal and not local issues.

37. Answer: a and d
Please note that we are looking for statements that are NOT true. Bicycle racks will NOT

help community connectivity. Retention ponds will reduce stormwater runoff.

38. Answer: b

    A construction waste management plan should include materials to be used for alternative daily cover (ADC). Answers "c" and "d" should be part of the design phase decisions. The recycling capacity of the neighborhood recycle center does NOT need to be part of the construction waste management plan.

39. Answer: c and d

    Using the system that can gain the most points for LEED makes sense, but is not mandated by USGBC. Asking a landlord for advice is not a good choice and is NOT professional; the project team should be the advisor for the landlord. Using the 40/60 rule is correct. The **40/60 rule for LEED**: if a LEED system applies to 40% or less of the project or spaces, do not use it; if a LEED system applies to 60% or more of the project or spaces, use it. In the end, the project team makes an independent and final decision.

    See "LEED Rating System Selection Policy" at the link below:

    http://www.usgbc.org/Docs/Archive/General/Docs10132.pdf

Read this <u>free</u> document <u>at least three times</u>, because it is VERY important, and explains when to use each LEED system.

40. Answer: a

    The project team cannot seek precertification as a marketing tool for funding and attracting tenants, because precertification is for the LEED BDC CS (Core and Shell) rating system or LEED Volume Program ONLY. If the project has a signed lease or LOI for at least 70% of the spaces, this is good, but NOT required by GBCI. GBCI also does NOT require the project to be located in a new neighborhood for LEED NC.

41. Answer: c

    The project team can gain a point under IN because this program provides <u>quantitative</u> performance improvements for environmental benefit, which is <u>substantially</u> better than typical sustainable practice, and is applicable to <u>other</u> projects. Answer "b" is incorrect because the recycling credit for MR involves the building occupants (not the general public), and is limited to the following materials only:

    <u>P</u>aper
    <u>C</u>ardboard
    <u>M</u>etal
    <u>G</u>lass
    <u>Pl</u>astics

Mnemonics: People **C**an **M**ake **G**reen **P**romises

42. Answer: c, d, and e
    Wind and biofuel are clean energy. Natural gas is pretty clean, but still generates air pollution.

43. Answer: b and d
    Using water efficient fixtures applies only to indoor water; using native plants applies only to outdoor water; using sub-meters can monitor water leakage, and applies to all three cases. Water saving education programs can help teach all building users to save water, and applies to all three cases as well.

44. Answer: c
    ROI is a return on investment; **life-cycle analysis** is used to analyze the environmental impact of a building over its lifetime; **life-cycle cost analysis** is used to analyze the cost/savings of a building over its lifetime; life-cycle saving analysis is a distracter, and this term does not exist.

45. Answer: a
    ASHRAE 55-2010 includes standards regarding major factors affecting human comfort, such as temperature, humidity, air speed, etc. **ASHRAE 62.1-2010** is related to natural ventilation; the Carpet and Rug

Institute's **Green Label Plus** program is in regards to carpet and rugs; Green Building Index is a sustainable building rating tool used in Malaysia.

46. Answer: d

    If you pass the LEED Green Associate Exam, you can use the LEED Green Associate title or logo per GBCI guidelines on your business card. This question is testing your knowledge about the different scope of work done by GBCI and USGBC, and the proper use of the LEED Green Associate title or logo. Per GBCI, LEED GA is never an approved abbreviation of the LEED Green Associate title or logo.

    I use LEED GA as part of this book's main title simply because it is more legible on Amazon.com than using the full LEED Green Associate title.

47. Answer: d

    Furniture containing VOCs will affect EQ. The "450 miles from the job site" is included as a distracter.

48. Answer: d

    Green building through a holistic design approach has no definite relationship to construction time, cost, or savings over a building's lifetime. The design approach does improve the synergy of LEED credits.

49. Answer: c
    The building's foot print = the first floor area = 168,000 sf/8 = 21,000 sf

50. Answer: a
    1 acre = 43,560 sf. The site coverage = the first floor area/site area = 21,000/43,560 = 48%. This question tests your basic construction knowledge: 1 acre = 43,560 sf and the concept of site coverage.

51. Answer: b
    FAR (Floor Area Ratio) = the total building area/total **buildable** site area = 168,000/43,560 = 386%. This question tests your basic construction knowledge: 1 acre = 43,560 sf.

    This question also tests your knowledge of USGBC's definition of FAR which is TOTALLY different from what we are used to in the construction industry. I think this one will throw many people off. It's a good trick.

    See USGBC Definitions at the link below:

    https://www.usgbc.org/ShowFile.aspx?DocumentID=5744

52. Answer: c
For a single building project, the perimeter of the LEED project is typically the project's boundary; for a multi-building project, the LEED project team can choose a portion of the project site to submit as the LEED project boundary.

53. Answer: d
Green roofs include vegetated roofs and light color reflective roofs. Light color reflective roofs are NOT landscape areas. Retention ponds and sidewalks are not considered landscape areas. The best answer is vegetated roofs.

54. Answer: b. ASHRAE Standard 55-2010
ASHRAE 62.1-2010 relates to both EQ and EA category. The other two standards relate to LEED EA category only.

55. Answer: c
All the other answers are hard costs (material costs).

56. Answer: c
USGBC is in charge of creating all reference guides and the related errata.

57. Answer: c
Pay attention to the word "typically."

58. Answer: a
Technical Advisory Group is the best answer. The LEED Administrator is a distracter. USGBC is no longer involved with building LEED certification. GBCI depends on the Technical Advisory Group for CIRs.

59. Answer: b
ASHRAE 62.1-2010 specifies minimum ventilation rates for IAQ Performance. See EAP: Minimum Energy Performance.

60. Answer: a
ASTM and USGBC do not publish GWP and ODP scores. The Global Climate Control Board does not exist.

61. Answer: c
Universal Energy Conservation Codes and Energy Rating Codes do not exist. IPC stands for International Plumbing Code.

62. Answer: c
High SRI value and albedo can help alleviate the heat island effect. Adding trees to a parking lot can reduce stormwater runoff to some extent, but grouping buildings together can reduce the hardscape areas, and is the most effective way to reduce stormwater runoff.

63. Answer: d
The qualified Basic Services that can help to

gain LEED points for community connectivity include, but are not limited to:
a) Place of Worship
b) Restaurant
c) Supermarket
d) Convenience Grocery
e) Laundry
f) Cleaner
g) Beauty Salon
h) Hardware
i) Pharmacy
j) Medical/Dental
k) Bank
l) Senior Care Facility
m) Community Center
n) Fitness Center
o) Daycare
p) School
q) Library
r) Museum
s) Theater
t) Park
u) Fire Station
v) Post Office

A shopping center includes many of the basic services listed above, and is the best choice.

64. Answer: c
A car powered by gas is a non-alternative-fuel vehicle

65. Answer: d
Answer "a" is considered carpooling; Answer "b" is simply sharing parking cost; and Answer "c" is a shuttle service program.

66. Answer: a
A project team does NOT need to certify everything inside the property boundary, and can determine the LEED project site boundary for LEED submittal and certification.

67. Answer: b
Per UPC, **graywater** is household water that has not come into contact with kitchen sinks, human excretion, or animal waste. Graywater includes used water from bathroom washbasins, bathtubs, showers, and water from laundry tubs and clothes washers. Graywater does not include water from dishwashers or kitchen sinks.

68. Answer: c
Cradle-to-cradle analysis is the same as life cycle analysis, eco-balance, or life cycle assessment, and is used to evaluate the environmental impact of a service or product. We use whole building perspective for LEED. Energy reduction is only one aspect of LEED. LEED includes other categories, such as SS, WE, EQ, etc. Integrated design approach is a design approach that includes consideration for

<u>people, planet and profit</u> (triple bottom line or three Ps).

69. Answer: a
CFC can be replaced with CO_2 or other refrigerants. Halons are used for fire suppression systems. The manufacture of HVAC units containing CFCs was stopped in the United States in 1995. These units had been phased out from existing buildings located in the United States by 2011.

70. Answer: a and e
SRI stands for Solar Reflectance Index. Albedo means solar reflectance.

71. Answer: b
RECs mean Renewable Energy Certificates. They represent positive attributes of power generated by renewable sources. When you purchase RECs, you are buying the attributes, NOT necessarily the real power used in your project. Anyone can purchase RECs from anywhere, even if the power used in his/her project is not green power. The money s/he pays allows others to generate or use green power, and achieves overall reduction of the use of fossil fuels in the world. This is a marketing approach for sustainability.

72. Answer: b and d
Per USGBC, the priorities for LEED projects are based on environmental

guidelines and project constraints.

73. Answer: c

    Burning construction waste on site is not acceptable. Answers "a" and "b" are good practice, but they cannot reduce <u>construction</u> waste.

74. Answer: d

    Prerequisites and credits are part of the LEED building rating systems, MPRs are Minimum Project Requirements, and the foundation of the LEED building rating systems is the triple bottom line, which means <u>people, profit, and planet</u>.

75. Answer: c

    The project cannot use LEED BDC NC certification because the building is less than 9 stories high. The project team should use the LEED BD+C: Homes and Multifamily Lowrise rating system instead.

76. Answer: d

    Per Montreal Protocol, the manufacture of HVAC units containing CFCs was stopped in the United States in 1995. These units had been phased out from existing buildings located in the United States by 2011. HCFCs, which are less active, have to be phased out by 2030.

77. Answer: b and c
   Grease typically goes down the drains in the kitchen as part of the blackwater. Toxic metal can be found in blackwater also. CO and halons are unlikely to be found in wastewater.

78. Answer: c
   Answer "a" is good practice, but is not the best choice; no matter how good a job you do, the system can still fail and leak out refrigerants. Answer "b" is partially correct; there are refrigerants without ODP (ozone depletion potential) that still have GWP (global warming potential). Answer "c" is the best choice; if you do not use refrigerants, there is absolutely no chance for them to leak out and cause environmental damage.

79. Answer: a and d
   The LEED project boundary only includes the portion of the site submitted by the project team for LEED certification, and does not necessarily overlap with the edge of the entire development, or the edge of the building. The boundary does include the entire project scope of work

80. Answer: b and d
   Reduced disturbance of wetlands is an environmental benefit, not necessarily an economic benefit. Increased use of rapidly

renewable materials may not save money. Better EQ does create fewer liabilities, lowers the cost related to employees' health, and reduces the number of employee sick days.

81. Answer: c and d
Biofuel is generated from plant material like crops, trees, and grasses. Gas and natural gas are both fossil fuels.

82. Answer: a
All other choices are good practice, but they do NOT necessarily need to be implemented for water efficiency.

83. Answer: a
This is the definition of durability.

84. Answer: b and c
The removal of refrigerants containing ODP and GWP should be conducted by a specialist, and is not part of a construction waste management plan. The reduction of building size is part of the design decision, not part of a construction waste management plan.

85. Answer: c and d
HCFCS and CFCs should not be used because of their ozone depletion potential (ODP).

86. Answer: b and d
Both answer "b" and "d" can earn points for Innovation.

87. Answer: c
The same strategy can be used for other projects, but it may or may not earn an IN point. Each case has to be reviewed and determined by GBCI.

88. Answer: b
NH3 has a lower GWP than HCFC.

For more information see: "**The Treatment by LEED of the Environmental Impact of HVAC Refrigerants**." You can download this PDF file for free at the link below:

http://www.gbci.org/Files/References/The-Treatment-by-LEED-of-the-Environmental-Impact-of-HVAC-Refrigerants.pdf

This is a VERY important document that you need to become familiar with. Many real LEED exam questions (CFC, HCFC, HFC, etc.) come from this document. You should download the file and read at least 3 times.

Pay special attention to the Table on ODP and GWP. You do not have to remember the exact value of all ODPs and GWPs, but you do need to know the rough number for various groups of refrigerants.

89. Answer: a and c
An educational program on LEED is the most common way to gain points under the Innovation category. Answer "c" may earn extra points for Exemplary Performance under the Innovation category. Answer "b" may help the project earn a higher level of LEED certification, but no other rewards.

90. Answer: a
Proper building orientation and fenestration can take full advantage of the dominant winds in the summer, and avoid chilly north winds in the winter. These characteristics can also take full advantage of passive heating from the sun in the winter, and avoid the westerly sun in the summer. This can be more efficient than ALL the HVAC equipment combined. There is no such thing as LEED certified equipment.

91. Answer: c
All LEED rating systems can have CIRs, including LEED ND.

92. Answer: b
ASHRAE standards do not apply to WE.

93. Answer: b
Rainwater is non-potable water. Please also see the definitions for blackwater and graywater in the explanations of Questions #9, #10, #32, and #67. Raw water is a

distracter.

94. Answer: b
    Prerequisites are the most important criteria for a LEED building rating system. They HAVE to be met before a building can earn LEED certification. Quantifiable performances, credits, and third party standards only apply to part of the LEED rating systems, and not ALL of them have to be met.

95. Answer: b and d
    Hardscape can reduce landscape area; mulches can prevent moisture loss. Both can reduce water for landscape irrigation. Perennials use more water. Overhead irrigation can increase water loss due to runoff and evaporation by the sun and wind. Head to head coverage is a standard practice for landscape irrigation.

96. Answer: a and d
    The following is true with regard to SSC: Heat Island Reduction? (Choose 2)
    - Temperatures in urban areas can be 22°F (12°C) higher than undeveloped areas and surrounding suburbs.
    - Measures to reduce heat islands measures include using a vegetated roof to insulate a building and extend the life of the roof or installing solar panels or shading devices.

Urban heat islands contribute to 24.2% (*not* 38.2. You do not need to memorize the exact percentage, but need to have a general idea) of regional warming according to a study of surface warming caused by rapid urbanization in east China.

The **solar reflectance index (SRI)** is the most effective measure of the ability of roofing materials to reject solar heat. However, in this credit, **solar reflectance (SR,** *not* SRI) is used to measure the solar heat rejection of "non-roof" materials or components that are not considered roofing materials, such as shading devices, vegetation, and other less reflective components.

97. Answer: d
Lightweight plants are most appropriate for a vegetated roof. Native plants or adaptive plants are good for LEED projects, but some of them are NOT appropriate for rooftops. A native tree with a large canopy on a vegetated roof means large roots will be present and may cause many problems.

98. Answer: b, d, and e
Consultation with an electrical engineer is good practice, but it is not as important as the other choices. The completion of the commissioning plan will occur AFTER

onsite renewable systems are selected.

99. Answer: c
    Scraps re-used from the same manufacture process, such as reground and rework, cannot be included as pre-consumer recycled items or post-consumer recycled items. Therefore, Answers "a" and "d" are incorrect. Demolition concrete pieces used at another project are salvaged materials.

100. Answer: e
    The project team can ONLY advise the school board that the LEED Platinum certification is achieved after the LEED application is reviewed and APPROVED by GBCI, because the GBCI can reject the application after the review or approve the project for a lower level of LEED certification.

II. Answers and Explanations for the LEED AP BD+C Mock Exam Part Two

If you answer 80 of the 100 questions correctly for a section, you have passed the mock exam for that section.

101. Answer: a, d and e

    With regard to submittals, the required documentation for Construction and Demolition Waste Management, Option 1 include:
    - MR Construction and Demolition Waste Management calculator or equivalent tool, tracking total and diverted waste amounts and material streams
    - Documentation of waste-to-energy facilities adhering to relevant EN standards (if applicable)
    - Documentation of recycling rates for commingled facilities (if applicable)

    Total waste per area (if applicable) is for Option 2.

    The following are distracters to confuse you:
    - A list of manufacturers' names, product names, costs, and percentage of pre- and post-consumer content (if applicable)
    - Manufacturers' letters or cutsheets indicating the listed products' recycled content (if applicable)
    - A plan showing the location of the

recycle area

102. Answer: d
Pay attention to the word "EXCEPT."

Building Life-Cycle Impact Reduction include the following options to achieve credits:
- Historic Building Reuse
- Renovation of Abandoned or Blighted Building
- Building and Material Reuse
- Whole-Building Life-Cycle Assessment

Whole-Building Reuse is not one of the option.

103. Answer: b and c
With regard to Minimum Indoor Air Quality Performance, the project team has the following options to obtain points:
- ASHRAE 62.1–2010 or a local equivalent, whichever is more stringent.
- CEN Standards EN 15251–2007 and EN 13779–2007

The following are distracters.
- ASHRAE Standard 170–2008
- Chartered Institution of Building Services Engineers (CIBSE) Applications Manual AM10

104. Answer: b and d

For a LEED v4 BD+C: New Construction project with 200 parking spaces, including 6 handicap parking spaces (1 of them is van accessible), the following statements are true with regard to Green Vehicles:

- The owner needs to designate 5% or 10 preferred parking spaces for fuel efficient and low emitting vehicles.
- The owner needs to provide electrical vehicle supply equipment (EVSE) or install liquid or gas alternative fuel fueling facilities or a battery switching station

105. Answer: b.

LEED BD+C: Core and Shell is the appropriate rating system to use if more than 40% of the gross floor area is incomplete at the time of certification

The USGBC has published a *LEED v4 User Guide* to assist you in choosing the right rating system for your project.

The **LEED BD+C** rating systems should be used for new construction or a major renovation with at least 60% of the project's gross floor area that must be complete by the time of certification (except for LEED BD+C: Core and Shell).

The USGBC uses a **40/60 rule** to assist you

when several rating systems seem to be acceptable for a project:

- Do not use a rating system if it is appropriate for less than 40% of the gross floor area of a LEED project building or space.
- Use a rating system if it is appropriate for more than 60% of the gross floor area of a LEED project building or space.
- A project team can decide which system to use if an appropriate rating system falls between 40% and 60% of the gross floor area.

See *LEED v4 User Guide* at the following link:
http://www.usgbc.org/sites/default/files/LEED%20v4%20User%20Guide_Final_0.pdf

106. Answer: d

MPRs are LEED's **Minimum Program Requirements**. A project must meet MPRs to qualify for LEED certification. One of the MPRs is that the building to site ratio must be 2% or higher. This project's building to site ratio is 1.5%, and therefore does not qualify for LEED certification.

107. Answer: d.

Only the project administrator has access to the CIR database and LEED Online after registration. As part of the registration, the

LEED project team will <u>have to</u> agree to report <u>post-occupancy water and energy use</u>. No credit will be awarded at the design submittal.

108. Answer: a
Homebuilders who intend to achieve LEED for Homes certification must contact a LEED for Homes provider organization (NOT a Green Rater, or an Energy Rater directly.).

For LEED for Homes, you need to deal with a LEED for Homes Provider, a Green Rater, and an Energy Rater.

A LEED for Homes Provider is the referee when it comes to who is able to be a **Green Rater** for a LEED for Homes project. The Provider is responsible for hiring, training, and overseeing the Green Raters. The USGBC requires that each Provider have a quality assurance protocol for its Green Raters. Homebuilders who intend to achieve LEED for Homes certification **<u>must</u> contact a LEED for Homes Provider** organization. Refer to the following link for a complete list of LEED for Homes Provider organizations in the United States:
http://www.usgbc.org/organizations/members/homes-providers

A Green Rater is a professional who has shown qualifications for energy rating certification, and demonstrates the ability to deal with a home's energy systems and performance. Certification can be obtained from accreditation bodies such as ENERGY STAR, RES NET, BPI, etc. Green Raters provide the required *on-site* verification.

An Energy Rater initiates a *performance* test which is mandatory for the LEED for Homes rating system. The largest body of energy raters is called **Home Energy Raters (HERS Raters).** The **Residential Energy Services Network (RES NET)** administers HERS Raters credentials.

109. Answer: a, c and d
 The following statements regarding LEED are true:
 - CIR stands for Credit Interpretation Rulings.
 - The USGBC will start to review your project 10 working days after receiving your submittal.
 - A Green Rater is a professional who has shown qualifications for an energy rating certification, and demonstrates abilities to deal with a home's energy systems and performance.

 Precertification is for LEED BD+C: Core and Shell ONLY, and not for LEED BD+C: New Construction.

With regard to LEED Certification, you have 25 business days (NOT 20 days) to appeal any comments from the USGBC. You need to pay $500 for each appealed credit (NOT each appeal).

110. Answer: c and d
 The following statements regarding CIRs are true:
 - Always review the GBCI and USGBC websites for previous CIRs before you submit one.
 - If you cannot find a similar CIR, then submit a new CIR to GBCI online.

 A CIR only provides feedback, and it will not guarantee a credit. After a CIR, you will know that you probably will get a credit but NOT for sure.

 If a LEED AP is not sure about where to place the handicap parking stalls, he can seek advice from the governing agencies, NOT the GBCI.

111. Answer: b and c
 The following statements regarding LTC: Reduced Parking Footprint are true:
 - Parking is expensive, and costs developers and landowners about $15,000 per space on average in the United States.

- Locating projects in mixed-use, high-density areas or in places well served by transit can reduce parking demand.

The following are incorrect:
- Asphalt and concrete parking lots cover about 35% of the surface area in the average nonresidential areas. (Asphalt and concrete parking lots cover about 50% to 70% of the surface area in the average nonresidential or 35% of the surface area in the average US residential neighborhood.)
- Preferred parking for carpools can increase parking demand. (Preferred parking for carpools can *reduce* parking demand.)

112. Answer: a and c
Pay attention to the word "not." So, the following are incorrect statements but the correct answers:
- The separation of the tasks for the USGBC and the GBCI is to meet the protocols of ASTM and ISO.
- A portable classroom building may qualify for LEED NC or LEED Schools.

The separation of the tasks for the USGBC and the GBCI meets the protocols of the American National Standard Institute (ANSI) and International Organization for Standardization (ISO). A building must be

1,000 s.f. minimum for LEED BD+C: New Construction, LEED BD+C: Core and Shell Development, LEED BD+C: Schools and LEED O+M. A LEED project must be a permanent and complete space or building. A LEED project must comply with environmental laws.

113. Answer: a and c
A building must be 250 s.f. minimum for LEED ID+C: Commercial Interiors.

The following statements are true:
- This project must meet ADA guidelines.
- This project can seek LEED ID+C: Commercial Interiors certification.

114. Answer: c and d
Pay attention to the word "not." So, the following are incorrect statements bit the correct answers:
- A LEED project team does not include product manufacturers.
- A LEED project team does not include structural engineers.

115. Answer: a, c and e
A project team needs to submit the following to achieve SS Prerequisite (SSP): Construction Activity Pollution Prevention for projects using local standards and codes:
- Drawings depicting erosion and sedimentation control measures

implemented
- Description of how project complies with local standards and codes
- Comparison of local standards and codes with EPA CGP

The following are distracters:
- A narrative detailing BMP and ESC and responsible parties.
- Field reports or shop drawing logs, product cut sheets, etc. (These are required for any typical project).

116. Answer: a and d

 SS Prerequisite (SSP): Construction Activity Pollution Prevention encourages project teams to reduce construction project disturbances to rainwater systems, the site itself, and neighboring properties. Local codes frequently control construction activity pollution; however, some governing agencies may not have such codes. LEED uses the US Environmental Protection Agency (EPA) **construction general permit (CGP)**, a US-based national standard, to guarantee that all projects implement **erosion and sedimentation control (ESC)** measures during construction.

 SS Prerequisite (SSP): Construction Activity Pollution Prevention may contribute to the following prerequisite or credits:
- SSC: Site Development—Protect or

Restore Habitat
- SSC: Rainwater Management

The following are distracters:
- SSC: Heat Island Reduction
- SSC: Open Space

This question tests your knowledge of synergy between different LEED prerequisites and credits. **Synergy** is the combined effects of two or more agents or forces greater than the sum of their individual.

117. Answer: a and d

    A site assessment identifies **assets**, such as good solar access, healthy plant populations, and favorable climate conditions, as well as **liabilities**, such as steep slopes, pollution sources, blighted structures, unhealthy soils, and extreme climate patterns. In a word, it assesses environmental features and assists the design of a sustainable site and building.

    SSC: Site Assessment may contribute to the following prerequisite or credits:
    - IPC: Integrative Process
    - EAC: Renewable Energy Production

    The following are distracters:
    - SSC: Light Pollution Reduction
    - EAC: Green Power and Carbon Offsets

118. Answer: c

This is a difficult question, and I purposely place it at the front portion of the exam to test you. On the real LEED exam, you may encounter very hard questions (or test content that you have NEVER read about before) at the front portion of the exam, your strategy must be NOT to waste too much time on these kinds of questions, eliminate the obvious wrong answers, and then do an educational guess and then move on. Mark it as a question that you need to review later and then come back to it again if you have time AFTER you finish ALL the questions. But, you may NOT have time to come back later, so do you best the first time, even when you are guessing.

The key to this question is that you need to know 1 acre = 43,560 s.f. I purposely do NOT give you this information in the main text of this book to let you have the experience of encountering something you have not read about.

To achieve SSC: Site Development—Protect or Restore Habitat, on previously graded or developed land, according to **Option 1, On-Site Restoration**, a project team needs to protect or restore at least 30% of the site area (including the building footprint).

30% × site area = 30% × 43,560 s.f. = 13,068 s.f.

So, the correct answer is c or 13,068 s.f. If you do not remember the exact number of 1 acre = 43,560 s.f., but have a rough idea, you still have a good chance of eliminating the two obvious wrong answers (a and b) and guessing the correct answer (50% chance).

Option 2 of SSC: Site Development—Protect or Restore Habitat is **Financial Support:** The project team needs to provide financial support equivalent to at least $0.40 per square foot (US$4 per square meter) for the total site area
(including the building footprint) to an approved nationally or locally recognized land trust or conservation organization.

The following is unnecessary information used as **distracters** to confuse you:
This is a 12,000 s.f., 2-story building. The building's first floor area is twice that of the second floor.

119. Answer: c
Unlike previous versions of LEED, LEED v4 allows products that are part of MEP (mechanical, electrical and plumbing) systems but are "passive" (meaning not part of the active portions of the system) to be

included in credit calculations, such as ducts, duct insulation, conduit, plumbing fixtures piping, pipe insulation, faucets, showerheads, and lamp housings. However, the LEED project team *must* exclude the existing MEP equipment in:

- MRC: Building Product Disclosure and Optimization—Sourcing of Raw Materials, Option 4. This Option specifically excludes mechanical and equipment electrical and controls, plumbing fixtures, fire detection and alarm system fixtures, elevators, and conveying systems.

The following are **distracters**:

- MR Prerequisite (MRP): Storage and Collection of Recyclables, Option 3
- MRP: Construction and Demolition Waste Management Planning, Option 2
- MRC: Building Life-Cycle Impact Reduction, Option 1

120. Answer: d

To achieve point(s) for MRC: Construction and Demolition Waste Management, a project needs to:

- divert 50% and Three Material Streams

OR

- generate not more than 2.5 pounds of construction waste per square foot

121. Answer: b
MRC: Building Life-Cycle Impact Reduction is related to most of the other credits. It is related to the following six credits:
- LTC: High-Priority Site
- MRP: Construction and Demolition Waste Management Planning
- MRC: Construction and Demolition Waste Management
- MRC: Building Product Disclosure and Optimization—Sourcing of Raw Materials
- MRC: Building Product Disclosure and Optimization—Environmental Product Declarations
- MRC: Building Product Disclosure and Optimization—Material Ingredients

MRP: Construction and Demolition Waste Management Planning is related to MRC: Construction and Demolition Waste Management.

MRC: Design for Flexibility is related to the following four credits:
- MRP: Construction and Demolition Waste Management Planning
- MRC: Building Product Disclosure and Optimization—Environmental Product Declarations
- MRC: Building Product Disclosure and Optimization—Sourcing of Raw Materials

- MRC: Building Product Disclosure and Optimization—Material Ingredients

122. Answer: b and d

    Pay attention to the word "not." We are looking for statements are not true. So, the following are incorrect statements but the correct answers:
    - Materials that are reused on-site are required to be repurposed.
    - Biobased materials are defined by the harvest cycle of the raw materials. (They must meet the Sustainable Agriculture Standard instead).

    The following are correct statements but the incorrect answers:
    - MRC: Rapidly Renewable Materials does not exist for LEED v4.
    - MR Credit Regional Materials. The 500-mile (805-km) radius requirement was decreased to 100 miles (160 km).

123. Answer: b and d

    To meet EQP: Environmental Tobacco Smoke Control, a LEED project team needs to submit the following for Option 2:
    - Any code or landlord restrictions that prevent establishment of no-smoking requirements.
    - Door schedule demonstrating weather-stripping at exterior unit doors and doors leading from units to common hallways

The following are distracters:
- Manufacturer's data sheets showing the air-tight properties of the partition
- Test results for air quality in non-smoking areas.

124. Answer: b

    Basis of Design (BOD) is NOT part of the minimum requirements for IP Prerequisite (IPP): Integrative Project Planning and Design.
    The following are the minimum requirements for this prerequisite:
    - Owner's Project Requirements (OPR) Document
    - Preliminary Rating Goals
    - Integrated Project Team
    - Design Charrette

125. Answer: c

    IP Prerequisite (IPP): Integrative Project Planning and Design applies to LEED BD+C: Healthcare rating system.

126. Answer: a and c

    To achieve LTC: Access to Quality Transit, the project must meet the following requirements:
    - The project shall be located within 1/4 mile of walking distance of existing or planned bus, streetcar, or rideshare stops, or within 1/2 mile of one planned and

funded, or one existing, bus rapid transit stops, light or heavy rail stations, commuter rail stations, or commuter ferry terminals.
- The transit service at those stops and stations in aggregate must meet a minimum number of trips.

All distances above can be measured from any functional entry of the project, and does not have to be from a main building entrance.

127. Answer: c
The following statements is true with regard to LTC: Access to Quality Transit:
- A project team can achieve a maximum of 6 Points for LEED BD+C: Core and Shell Development

128. Answer: a and d
This a tricky answer and answer. The key is to know there is a prerequisite and a credit for Outdoor Water Use Reduction. A prerequisite is mandatory for ALL projects.

The following statements are true with regard to Outdoor Water Use Reduction:
- All projects using a LEED BD+C rating system MUST achieve Outdoor Water Use Reduction.
- A project using a LEED BD+C rating system can achieve 2 points maximum through Outdoor Water Use Reduction.

129. Answer: a and c

The key is to know there is a prerequisite and a credit for water metering.

The following statements are true with regard to Water Metering:
- All projects using a LEED BD+C rating system MUST perform water metering. (WEP: Building-Level Water Metering)
- A project team can achieve points for water metering. (WEC: Water Metering)

130. Answer: a and d

Please pay attention to the word "not"

The following statements are *not* true with regard to Cooling Tower Water Use:
- Cooling Tower Water Use is applicable for LEED BD+C: Healthcare projects only.
- A project team can achieve a maximum of 3 Point for Cooling Tower Water Use

The following statements are true with regard to Cooling Tower Water Use:
- Cooling Tower Water Use is applicable for all LEED BD+C rating systems.
- A project team can achieve a maximum of 2 Point for Cooling Tower Water Use

131. Answer: c and d

For this question, "may" is the key word. Items a and b are ALL required (NOT optional) for this credit.

Per the USGBC reference guide:
"Systems that *must* be commissioned for this prerequisite include the following:
- Mechanical, including HVAC&R equipment and controls
- Plumbing, including domestic hot water systems, pumps, and controls
- Electrical, including service, distribution, lighting, and controls, including daylighting controls
- Renewable energy systems"

132. Answer: b and d

    Pay attention to the word "not."
    The following is not true regarding EQC: Low-Emitting Materials:
    - VOCs are from human-made materials only. (VOCs are from many sources: human made, natural, plant-based, and from people and animals.)
    - Compared with VOC content limits, air concentration measurements from chamber testing predict emissions over time better, and can provide better protection for installers. (Chamber emissions testing cannot evaluate emissions during installation, is less widely used for wet-applied products, and *cannot* provide better protection for installers.)

    The following are true statements, and

therefore the incorrect answers:
- It is related to CARB. (All paints and coatings wet-applied on site must meet the applicable VOC limits of the **South Coast Air Quality Management District (SCAQMD)** Rule 1113, effective June 3, 2011, or the **California Air Resources Board (CARB)** 2007, Suggested Control Measure (SCM) for Architectural Coatings.)
- This credit tackles each layer of the interior finish

133. Answer: a and c

 The following is true with regard to LTC: Sensitive Land Protection: (Choose 2)
 - It is related to LTC: Surrounding Density and Diverse Uses.
   - Selecting a site that has previously been developed and limiting the building's footprint to the previously developed area is one strategy to lessen the environmental consequences of a building.

 The following are incorrect:
 - A project tam can gain a maximum of 3 points for this credit, including 1 point for Exemplary Performance. (This credit has *no* Exemplary Performance. A project tam can gain a maximum of **2** points for LEED BD+C: Core and Shell, and 1 point

for other rating systems)
- Agricultural land conversion increases local opportunities to produce food. (Agricultural land conversion *limits* local opportunities to produce food.)

134. Answer: a and b

    The following statements are *not* true with regard to EAC: Optimize Energy Performance:
    - A project team can *only* use the Prescriptive Compliance Method to achieve points for LEED BD+C: New Construction and LEED BD+C: Core and Shell.
    - A project team can *only* use the Whole Building Energy Simulation Method to achieve points for LEED BD+C: New Construction and LEED BD+C: Core and Shell.

    The truth is a project team can use either the Prescriptive Compliance Method or the Whole Building Energy Simulation Method.

135. Answer: b

    The highest level of building LEED certification they can achieve for this project is Silver.

    The USGBC has four levels of building certification. The four levels and the points required for each are as follows:

Certified	**40**–49	points
Silver	**50**–59	points
Gold	**60**–79	points
Platinum	**80**	points and above

The level achieved by a building is based on the number of points earned under the LEED green building rating system. The points are calculated using the scorecards or checklists provided by the USGBC.

No matter which **LEED v4.0** rating system you choose, each LEED v4.0 rating system has **100** base points; a maximum of **6** possible extra points for Innovation (IN), and a maximum of **4** possible extra points for Regional Priority (RP) for each project. There are 6 possible RP points, but you can only pick and choose a maximum of 4 points for each project.

Refer to the following link for the **Regional Priority Credits (RPC)** for all 50 States. With this spreadsheet, you can locate the RPC for your area by zip code:
http://www.usgbc.org/rpc

136. Answer: b
EAC: Renewable Energy Production Energy is typically handled at the Schematic Design phase

137. Answer: b, c and d
EAC: Optimize Energy Performance is typically handled at design phase, and not handled at the following project phases:
- Design Development
- Construction
- Construction Administration

138. Answer: a
The maximum points the project can get are: 1 point for IP, 2 points for LT, 5 points for SS, 9 points for WE, 8 points for EA, 6 points for MR, 8 points for EQ.

1 + 2 + 5 + 9 + 8 + 6 + 8 = 39 points

Plus a maximum of 5 possible extra points for Innovation (IN), and a maximum of 4 possible extra points for Regional Priority (RP) for each project:
39 +5 +4 = 48 points < 50 points

So, the highest level of building LEED certification they can achieve for this project is Certified.

139. Answer: a and d
With regard to EAC: Renewable Energy Production, the following may be Eligible Renewable Energy Systems:
- Wind energy systems
- Geothermal heating systems (in some

cases)

Other Eligible Renewable Energy Systems include:
- Photovoltaic
- Solar thermal
- Biofuel (in some cases)
- Low-impact hydroelectricity
- Wave and tidal energy

140. Answer: c and d
With regard to EAC: Renewable Energy Production, the following are definitely ineligible on-site systems:
- Passive solar
- Daylighting

Per the USGBC reference guide:
"Strategies like architectural features, passive solar, and daylighting, for example, reduce energy consumption but are not eligible renewable energy systems."

Some biofuels are eligible, but the following biofuels are ineligible:
- Combustion of municipal solid waste
- Forest biomass waste other than mill residue
- Wood coated with paints, plastics, or laminate
- Wood treated for preservation with materials containing chlorine compounds, chromated copper arsenate,

halogens, halide compounds, or arsenic; if more than 1% of the wood fuel has been treated with these compounds, the energy system is ineligible

141. Answer: a and c. They key word for this question is *"incorrect."* This credit <u>may</u> award a maximum of 1 point for all LEED BD+C rating systems, but we are looking for the statements that are <u>incorrect</u>, so a and c are the correct <u>answers</u>.

142. Answer: b and c

    With regard to EAC: Enhanced Refrigerant Management, the following are correct:
    - The credit is related to EAC: Optimize Energy Performance.
    - Do not use fire suppression systems containing ozone-depleting substances like Halons, CFCs, and HCFCs.

    The following are incorrect:
    - Small water coolers, small HVAC units, standard refrigerators, and other cooling equipment containing less than *1.5* lbs. of refrigerant are not included as part of the base building system and are exempt from this credit's requirements. (**Note:** Small systems with less than *0.5* pound (225 grams) of refrigerants, such as individual water fountains or stand-alone refrigerators, do not need to be included in credit calculations.

- For more than one type of equipment, use a weighted average of all base building HVAC&R equipment based on cost. (**Note:** It is based on *capacity* instead of *cost*)

143. Answer: a and c

    With regard to SSC: Tenant Design and Construction Guidelines, the following are correct:
    - The project team may need to submit a guideline on tenant's energy use, including information on how to determine energy use and the related costs.
    - The project team needs to show and update the locations of any meters for measurement on a diagram.

    The following are incorrect:
    - The project team may not need an IPMVP-compliant M&V plan.
    - The project team may not need to show and update the locations of any meters for measurement on a diagram.

144. Answer: c

    International Performance Measure and Verification Protocol (IPMVP) used in SSC: Tenant Design and Construction Guidelines.

145. Answer: a and c

    EAC: Green Power and Carbon Offsets is related to

- Green-e Energy
- Center for Resource Solution (CRS)

The following are incorrect answers:
- Green Label Plus (It is a Carpet and Rug Institute program, used as a distracter here)
- ASHRAE

146. Answer: a and c

    Pay attention to the word "incorrect."

    The following are *incorrect* statements but *correct* answers:
    - Paper, food, metals, glass, and plastics make up about 50% of the total municipal solid waste stream. (It should be 60%)
    - The GBCI encourages you to compost food scraps and yard trimmings of waste on-site if possible.

    The following are *correct* statements but *incorrect* answers:
    - Based on percentage of weight, the remaining solid waste's ranking from highest to lowest is yard trimmings, textiles, leather, rubber and other, and wood.
    - Yard trimmings cannot be composted on-site

147. Answer: a and d

    The following are true with regard to MRC: Building Product Disclosure and

Optimization—Sourcing of Raw Materials:
- Products sourced from manufacturers with self-declared reports are valued as *one half of* a product for credit achievement.
- ISO 26000: 2010 Guidance on Social Responsibility is part of the acceptable CSR frameworks

ASTM is NOT part of the acceptable CSR frameworks.

148. Answer: b and c
MRC: Design for Flexibility applies to LEED BD+C: Health Care *only*, and is related to the following credits:
- MRP: Construction and Demolition Waste Management Planning
- MRC: Building Product Disclosure and Optimization—Environmental Product Declarations

It is not related to the following:
- MRC: Building Life-Cycle Impact Reduction
- MRC: Furniture and Medical Furnishings

149. Answer: a and d
A project team can get one innovation point for MRC: Building Product Disclosure and Optimization—Material Ingredients by:
- Purchasing at least 40 permanently installed building products that meet the

credit criteria.
- Purchasing at least 50%, by *cost*, of permanently installed building products that meet the credit criteria.

150. Answer: d

    MRC: Building Product Disclosure and Optimization—Material Ingredients is related to GreenScreen. See the following link:

    cleanproduction.org/Greenscreen.v1-2.php

    The following are distracters:
    - ISO
    - ASTM
    - ASHRAE

151. Answer: b and c

    The following are *incorrect* statements, and therefore the *correct* answers:
    - A maximum of 2 points can be awarded for MRC: Building Life-Cycle Impact Reduction for LEED BD+C: Core and Shell. (It should be 6 points.)
    - A maximum of 6 points can be awarded for MRC: Building Product Disclosure and Optimization—Environmental Product Declarations for LEED BD+C: New Construction. (It should be 2 points.)

    You do not need memorize all the details, but you do need to have a rough idea of how many points you may get for each credit.

152. Answer: d
MRC: PBT Source Reduction—Lead, Cadmium, and Copper is typically handled at Construction Documents project phase. A project team can specify materials that is free of Lead, Cadmium, and Copper at this phase.

153. Answer: c and d
The followings are pre-consumer materials:
- Materials from regrind
- Materials from rework

154. Answer: b
MR building product disclosure and optimization calculator or equivalent tracking tool *must* be included in the LEED submittal package for MRC: Building Product Disclosure and Optimization—Sourcing of Raw Materials for both Options 1 & 2.

Corporate sustainability reports for 100% of products contributing toward credit is only required for Option 1, not for Option 2.

The following are distracters:
- A list of actual materials costs
- A list of manufacturers' names and manufacturers' letters or cutsheets
- The percentage of recycled materials by volume

155. Answer: a

For a LEED BD+C: New Construction project, MRC: Building Product Disclosure and Optimization—Material Ingredients, Option 2, Material Ingredient Optimization is based on cost.

156. Answer: b

A contractor is working on a LEED BD+C: New Construction project. He can achieve a maximum of 2 points for MRC: Furniture and Medical Furnishings.

157. Answer: a

For a LEED BD+C: New Construction project, a project team can achieve 0 point for Construction and Demolition Waste Management Planning because it is a prerequisite, not a credit.

158. Answer: a

EAP: Fundamental Commissioning and Verification is related to EAC: Demand Response.

The following are distracters:
- EAP: Minimum Energy Performance
- EAC: Renewable Energy Production
- EAC: Green Power and Carbon Offsets

159. Answer: c

A retail project can choose EAP: Minimum

Energy Performance, Option 3, Prescriptive Compliance: Advanced Buildings™ Core Performance™ Guide.

Per the USGBC reference guide:
"To be eligible for Option 3, the project must be less than 100,000 square feet (9,290 square meters).

Note: Healthcare, Warehouse or Laboratory projects are ineligible for Option 3."

160. Answer: a, b and c
 The following are related to MRC: Building Product Disclosure and Optimization—Material Ingredients, Option 1, Material Ingredient Reporting:
 - Chemical Abstract Service Registration Number (CASRN)
 - Health Product Declaration
 - Cradle to Cradle
 - GreenScreen
 - USGBC approved program

 EPA is a distracter.

161. Answer: c
 MRC: Building Product Disclosure and Optimization—Material Ingredients, Option 3, Product Manufacturer Supply Chain Optimization, the document of the ingredients used to make the building

product or building material is based on weight.

Per the USGBC reference guide:
"Use building products for at least 25%, by *cost*, of the total value of permanently installed products in the project that:
- Are sourced from product manufacturers who engage in validated and robust safety, health, hazard, and risk programs which at a minimum document at least 99% (by *weight*) of the ingredients used to make the building product or building material, and…"

162. Answer: b
Pay attention to the word "must."

With regard to EQP: Minimum Indoor Air Quality Performance, a LEED project team *must* submit the following no matter which option you choose:
- Controls drawing showing monitoring devices

The following are required for Options 1 & 2, as well as Mixed Mode, but not required for Naturally Ventilated:
- Confirmation that project meets minimum requirements of ASHRAE 62.1–2010, Sections 4–7
- Confirmation that project has MERV 11 or higher filters

- Ventilation rate procedure

163. Answer: b
The Project Phase for EQP: Minimum Indoor Air Quality Performance is design phase.

Schematic Design Phase is too early for this prerequisite, while Construction Phase is too late.

164. Answer: a
EQP: Environmental Tobacco Smoke Control is typically handled at the Pre-Design project phases.

All the other project phases are too late for this prerequisite
- Schematic Design
- Design Development
- Construction Documents
- Construction Administration
- Occupation/Operation

165. Answer: d
With regard to synergies, EQP: Environmental Tobacco Smoke Control is *not* related to any prerequisite and credit. This is an interesting new change for LEED v4.

166. Answer: a and b
Pay attention to the word "not."

The following are *not* the responsible parties for IEQp3: Minimum Acoustical Performance:
- The Contractor
- The Civil Engineer, Environmental Engineer, or Geotechnical Engineer

The following are the responsible parties for IEQp3: Minimum Acoustical Performance:
- Mechanical Engineer
- Architect

167. Answer: a and d
 A LEED project team uses fly ash in concrete mixes. The following statements are true:
 - The LEED project team may seek an Innovation Credit (INC) point because this is a reuse of pre-consumer content.
 - The design team needs to get the owner's consent for using the fly ash.

 Innovation Credit (INC) encourages projects to achieve innovative, pilot or exceptional performance.

168. Answer: c, e and g
 EQC: Indoor Air Quality Assessment is related to the following Referenced Standards:
 - ASTM
 - ISO
 - U.S. EPA
 - Volatile Organic Compounds

- California Department of Public Health

The following are distracters:
- ANSI
- ASHRAE
- Carbon Trust
- International Performance Measure and Verification Protocol (IPMVP)

169. Answer: b and c
With regard to synergies, EQC: Construction Indoor Air Quality Management Plan is related to the following:
- EQC: Low-Emitting Materials
- EQC: Indoor Air Quality Assessment

The following are distracters:
- EAP: Minimum Energy Performance
- EAC: Enhanced Commissioning
- EAC: Green Power and Carbon Offsets

170. Answer: b and c
Pay attention to the word "not."

With regard to EQC: Construction Indoor Air Quality Management Plan, the following are not true:
- A project team can seek 2 points for this credit.
- It does not apply to LEED BD+C: Core and Shell.

The following are true:
- A project team can seek 1 point for this credit.
- It applies to LEED BD+C: Core and Shell.

In fact, it applies to all 8 LEED BD+C rating systems:
- LEED BD+C: New Construction
- LEED BD+C: Core and Shell
- LEED BD+C: Schools
- LEED BD+C: Retail
- LEED BD+C: Data Center
- LEED BD+C: Warehouse and Distribution Center
- LEED BD+C: Hospitality
- LEED BD+C: Health Care

171. Answer: a, c and e

    A project team is working on a LEED NC project. The following can qualify as a basic service for LTC: Surrounding Density and Diverse Uses:
    - A Chinese restaurant
    - An Olive Garden restaurant
    - A Ralph's Supermarket

    The following do not qualify as a basic service:
    - A law office with 20 employees
      Note: *Commercial office needs to have*

100 or more full-time equivalent jobs to qualify.
- A public restroom

The USGBC reference guide, Appendix 1 has a list of qualified basic service. It includes five categories:
- Food retail
- Community-serving retail
- Services
- Civic and community facilities
- Community anchor uses (BD+C and ID+C only)

Each categories is further divided into various services.

Per the USGBC, the following restrictions apply:
"A use counts as only one type (e.g., a retail store may be counted only once even if it sells products in several categories).

No more than two uses in each use type may be counted (e.g. if five restaurants are within walking distance, only two may be counted).

The counted uses must represent at least three of the five categories, exclusive of the building's primary use."

172. Answer: d
    The maximum number of points that you can

earn for LEED BD+C: Core and Shell Development or any other LEED rating systems is 110 points.

No matter which **LEED v4** rating system you choose, each LEED v4.0 rating system has a maximum of 110 points, including **100** base points, a maximum of **6** possible extra points for Innovation (IN), and a maximum of **4** possible extra points for Regional Priority (RP) for each project. There are 6 possible RP points, but you can only pick and choose a maximum of 4 points for each project.

See U.S. Green Building Council. *LEED v4 for Building Design and Construction Checklist*. U.S. Green Building Council, 2013.
http://www.usgbc.org/resources/leed-v4-building-design-and-construction-checklist

173. Answer: b
All LEED rating systems, including LEED v4 BD+C: Schools, have the following levels of certifications: LEED-CERTIFIED, LEED-SILVER, LEED-GOLD, and LEED-PLATINUM

174. Answer: d
There are 9 credit categories for LEED v4 BD+C: New Construction. They are Integrative Process (IP), Location and Transportation (LT), Sustainable Sites (SS),

Water Efficiency (WE), Energy and Atmosphere (EA), Materials and Resources (MR), Indoor Environmental Quality (EQ), Innovation (IN), and Regional Priority (RP).

Please note LEED v4 has changed IEQ to EQ.

175. Answer: a
The USGBC released LEED v4 at the GreenBuild International Conference and Expo in November 2013. The GBCI started to include the new LEED v4 content for all LEED exams in late Spring 2014. We have incorporated the new LEED v4 content in this book.

176. Answer: b and c
Pay attention to the word "not."

The following is not true regarding SSC: Rainwater Management:
- Low-impact development disrupt the natural water flow and water balance.
- The best way to manage rainwater is to pipe and convey runoff into large, centralized facilities at the base of drainage areas as quickly as possible.

The following is true regarding SSC: Rainwater Management, and therefore not the correct answers:
- Conventional site development uses soil

compaction.
- Green infrastructure (GI) rainwater management strategies and techniques mimic a site's natural hydrology, and improve upon the conventional approach. Project teams treat rainwater as a resource instead of a waste product.

177. Answer: d

Pay attention to the word "not."
A flood basin cannot be a High-Priority Site.

A flood basin can be a High-Priority Site, and therefore the incorrect answer.
- A Historic District
- A Federal Empowerment Zone site
- A Brownfield

178. Answer: d

Equipment Vendor is not involved in green building design.

179. Answer: a and b

The following are related to MRC: PBT Source Reduction—Mercury:
- MRC: Building Life-Cycle Impact Reduction
- MRC: Building Product Disclosure and Optimization—Environmental Product Declarations

The following are distracters:
- MRC: PBT Source Reduction—Lead,

Cadmium, and Copper
- MRC: Demolition Waste Management

180. Answer: c

For LEED v4 BD+C: New Construction or any other LEED rating systems, 50 points are needed for Silver Certification.

No matter which **LEED v4** rating system you choose, the USGBC has four levels of building certification. The four levels and the points required for each are as follows:

Certified	**40**–49	points
Silver	**50**–59	points
Gold	**60**–79	points
Platinum	**80**	points and above

The level achieved by a building is based on the number of points earned under the LEED green building rating system. The points are calculated using the scorecards or checklists provided by the USGBC.

181. Answer: d

For Construction Activity Pollution Prevention, ESC stands for Erosion and Sedimentation Control.

182. Answer: c

For LEED v4 BD+C: New Construction, Surrounding Density and Diverse Uses, you need to construct a building that meets density requirements within a ¼ mile walking distance AND has a certain number of diverse uses within a 1/2 mile walking distance of the site.

LEED v4 has changed the criteria from "radius" to "walking distance."

183. Answer: d

To get point(s) for Access to Quality Transit, your building needs to be:
- Located within ½ mile of a subway or rail station that provides a minimum number of trips.
AND
- Located within ¼ mile of one or more bus stops for two or more bus lines that provide a minimum number of trips.

184. Answer: a and c

You can get one point for Bicycle Facilities by locating the project such that:
- a functional entry or bicycle storage is within a 200-yard walking distance
OR
- a functional entry or bicycle storage is within a 200-yard bicycling distance from a bicycle network that connects to at least one of the diverse uses

185. Answer: a

You can get three points for Optimize Energy Performance by improving a new building's energy performance by 10%.

See Energy and atmosphere credit (EAC): Optimize Energy Performance

186. Answer: d
 The following is true with regard to EQC: Quality Views:
 - 75% of all regularly occupied floor area must have at least two of the four qualified kinds of views

 The following statements are not true:
 - LEED BD+C: Health Care projects can get a maximum of 5 points for this credit (It should be 32points)
 - Up to 20% of the required area with access to quality views can now be into atriums. (It should be 30%)
   - View glazing in the contributing area can have frits. (Frits, fibers, patterned glazing, or added tints that distort color balance)

187. Answer: a and c
 The following are true with regard to EQC: Daylight:
 - Daylight reinforces circadian rhythms.
 - This credit is related to EAP: Minimum Energy Performance and EA Credit Optimize Energy Performance.

 The following are not true:

- This credit has advanced greatly and now focuses on using **actual measurement** and **window design** to approximate daylight levels and daylight quality. (It should be **simulated daylight analysis** instead of **window design**.)
- This credit is related to SSC: Light Pollution Reduction

188. Answer: c and d
With regard to synergies, SSC: Open Space, is related to the following:
- SSC: Heat Island Reduction
- SSC: Site Assessment

The following are distracters:
- WEC: Outdoor Water Use Reduction
- WEC: Water Metering

189. Answer: a
With regard to SSC: Open Space, the project team can achieve 0 point.

Per the USGBC reference guide, the project need to meet the following criteria to achieve 1 point for this credit:
"Provide outdoor space greater than or equal to 30% of the total site area (including building footprint). A minimum of 25% of that outdoor space must be vegetated (turf grass does not count as vegetation) or have overhead vegetated canopy."

The total site area is one acre = 43,560 s.f.
Note: It is important for you to know one acre = 43,560 s.f. This is a common conversion that is used in almost every project.

The outdoor space is 15,000 s.f.

15,000 s.f./ 43,560 s.f. = 34% > 30% required outdoor space

However, the outdoor space includes 8,000 s.f. of turf grass, and turf grass does *not* count as vegetation. So, the *potential* vegetated outdoor space = 15,000 s.f. - 8,000 s.f. = 7,000 s.f.

7,000 s.f/. 43,560 s.f. = 16% < 25% required vegetated outdoor space. So, this project does *not* meet the SSC: Open Space criteria, and will get 0 point for this credit.

190. Answer: d
 Pay attention to the word "not."

 The following is *not* true with regard to SSC: Places of Respite:
 - Options for shade or indirect sun must be provided, with at least one seating space per 300 square feet (27.8 square meters) of each respite area, with one wheelchair space per five seating spaces.

The following are true:
- Schools projects cannot achieve point for this credit. (SSC: Places of Respite only applies to LEED BD+C: Health Care)
- The area must be accessible from within the building or located within 200 feet (60 meters) of a building entrance or access point.
- The project team must provide additional dedicated places of respite for staff, equal to 2% of the net usable program area of the building.

191. Answer: a and c

    Chartered Institution of Building Service Engineers (CIBSE) is related to the following:
    - EQC: Interior Lighting
    - EQC: Enhanced Indoor Air Quality Strategies

    The following are distracters:
    - EAP: Minimum Energy Performance
    - EAC: Enhanced Commissioning

192. Answer: a and b

    Pay attention to the word "not."
    ASTM is not related to the following:
    - LTC: Reduced Parking Footprint
    - LTC: Green Vehicles

    The following are related to ASTM, and therefore the incorrect answers:

- EQC: Low-Emitting Materials
- EQC: Thermal Comfort

193. Answer: a and c

The following are true with regard to EQC: Thermal Comfort:

- Thermal comfort is a complex amalgam of six primary factors including surface temperature, air temperature, air movement, humidity, metabolic rate, and clothing.
- Predicted percentage of dissatisfied (PPD) and predicted mean vote (PMV) are two indices used as the referenced standards for this credit.

Research administered by the International Centre for Indoor Environment and Energy indicates allowing occupants +/–5°F (NOT +/–3°F) of local temperature control can give rise to productivity gains of 2.7% to 7%.

194. Answer: b and d

Pay attention to the word "not."

The following are not true with regard to SSC: Light Pollution Reduction:

- A project team *must* use backlight, uplight, and glare (BUG) rating method to achieve point(s) for this credit. (BUG rating method is one of the two methods, the other one is **calculation method**.)
- Illuminating Engineering Society and International Dark Sky Association

(IES/IDA) Model Lighting Ordinance (MLO) User Guide and IES TM-15-11, Addendum A: ies.org is one of the two reference standards. (It is the *only* reference standard for this credit.)

The following are true, and therefore the incorrect answers:
- When exposed to light pollution, some fauna and flora cannot adjust to seasonal variations.
- Reducing uplight, glare, and light trespass can contribute to good lighting design.

195. Answer: a and c

Advanced Buildings™ Core Performance™ Guide by New Buildings Institute is related to the following:
- EAP: Minimum Energy Performance
- EAC: Enhanced Commissioning

The following are distracters:
- EAP: Fundamental Refrigerant Management
- EAC: Green Power and Carbon Offsets

196. Answer: c

ASHRAE 52.2-2007 is related to EQC: Construction Indoor Air Quality Management Plan. There are several ASHRAE standards used in LEED, you need to know ASHRAE *52.2* is regarding *IAQ*.

The following are distracters:
- EAP: Minimum Energy Performance
- EQC: Acoustic Performance
- EQC: Thermal Comfort

197. Answer: d
ASHRAE Standard *55*-2010 is related to EQC: *Thermal* Comfort

The following are distracters:
- EAP: Minimum Energy Performance
- EQC: Acoustic Performance
- EQC: Construction Indoor Air Quality Management Plan

198. Answer: a, b and c

ASHRAE *62.1*-2010 is related to the following:
- EA EAP: Fundamental *Commissioning* and Verification
- EAP: Building-Level *Energy* Metering
- EQP: Minimum *Indoor* Air Quality Performance

The following are distracters:
- EQC: Acoustic Performance
- EQC: Interior Lighting

199. Answer: a and b
ASHRAE/IESNA Standard *90.1*-2007 is

related to the following:
- EAP: Minimum *Energy* Performance
- EAC: Optimize *Energy* Performance

The following are distracters:
- EQP: Minimum Indoor Air Quality Performance
- EQC: Indoor Air Quality Assessment

200. Answer: a and d
 ANSI is related to the following:
 - IPP: Integrative Project Planning and Design
 - EAP: Minimum Energy Performance

 The following are distracters:
 - WEC: Outdoor Water Use Reduction
 - WEC: Indoor Water Use Reduction

III. How were the LEED AP BD+C mock exams created?

The actual LEED AP BD+C Exam has 200 questions (100 questions for each section) and you must finish it within four hours. The raw exam score is converted to a scaled score ranging from 125 to 200. The passing score is 170 or higher.

I tried to be scientific when selecting the mock exam questions, so I based the number of questions for each credit category roughly on the number of points that you can get for that category. The level difficulty for each question was designed to match the official sample questions that can be downloaded from the official GBCI website. Feedback from our readers has indicated that this mock exam is relatively easy when compared to the actual LEED AP BD+C Exam.

IV. Where can I find the latest and official sample questions for the LEED AP BD+C Exam?

Answer: You can find them, as well as the exam content, from the candidate handbook, at:
http://www.usgbc.org/resources/leed-v4-ap-bdc-candidate-handbook

V. Latest trend for LEED exams

Recently, there are quite a few readers run into the versions of the LEED exams that have many questions on refrigerants (CFC, HCFC, and HFC), the following advice will help you answer these questions correctly:

For more information, see free pdf file of "The Treatment by LEED of the Environmental Impact of HVAC Refrigerants" that you can download at link below:

gbci.org/Files/References/The-Treatment-by-LEED-of-the-Environmental-Impact-of-HVAC-Refrigerants.pdf

This is a VERY important document that you need to become familiar with. Many real LEED exam questions (CFC, HCFC, and HFC, etc.) come from this document. You need to download it for free and read it at least 3 times.

Pay special attention to the Table on ODP and GWP on page 3. You do not have to remember the exact value of all ODPs and GWPs, but you do need to know the rough number for various groups of refrigerants."

This latest trend regarding refrigerants (CFC, HCFC, and HFC) for LEED Exams has a lot to do with LEED v4 Credit Weighting. EA (including refrigerants) is a big winner in LEED v4, meaning the category has MORE questions than any other areas for ALL the LEED exams. See portion of my book, *LEED GA Exam Guide* quoted below:

How are LEED credits allocated and weighted?

Answer: Credits that can contribute to LEED's **"Impact Categories"** are given more points. These impact categories are weighted through a consensus driven process and are as follows:
* global **climate change** (35%)
* social equity, environmental justice, and **community** quality of life (5%)
* individual **human health** and well-being (20%)
* **greener economy** (5%)
* **biodiversity** and Ecosystem (10%)
* **water resources** (15%)
* sustainable and regenerative **material resources** cycles (10%)

The USGBC uses three **association factors** to measure and scale credit outcome to a given impact category component.
1) **Relative efficacy** measures whether a credit outcome has a positive or negative association with a given Impact Category component, and how strong that association is. They're rated as follows:
    * no association
    * low association

- medium association
- high association
- negative association

2) **Benefit duration** measures how long the benefits or consequences of the credit outcome will last:
   - 1-3 Years
   - 4-10 Years
   - 11-30 Years
   - 30+ Years (Building/Community Lifetime)

3) **Controllability of effect** indicates which individual is most directly responsible for achieving the expected credit outcome. The more a credit outcome depends on active human effort, the less likely it will be achieved with certainty, and the credit will have fewer points. Less human effort equals more points.

The USGBC simplifies the weighting process of points into a **scorecard computed as follows**:
- **100 base points** for the base LEED Rating System
- **1 point minimum** for each credit
- **whole points** and no fractions for LEED points

See detailed discussions in the FREE PDF file entitled "LEED v4 Impact Category and Point

Allocation Development Process" at the following link:
http://www.usgbc.org/sites/default/files/LEED%20v4%20Impact%20Category%20and%20Point%20Allocation%20Process_Overview_0.pdf

VI. LEED AP BD+C Exam registration

1. **How to register for the LEED AP BD+C Exam?**
   Answer: Per the GBCI, you must create an Eligibility ID at www.GBCI.org. Select "My Credentials", and then select "Register for an exam" from your "Current Options," and you will find detailed instructions on how to set up an exam time and date with Prometric. You can reschedule or cancel the LEED AP BD+C Exam at www.prometric.com/gbci with your Prometric-issued confirmation number for the exam. You need to bring two forms of ID to the exam site. See www.prometric.com/gbci for a list of exam sites. Call 1-800-795-1747 (within the US) or 202-742-3792 (Outside of the US) or e-mail exam@gbci.org if you have any questions.

2. **Important Note:**
   You can download the "LEED AP BD+C Candidate Handbook" from the GBCI website and get all the latest details and procedures. Ideally you should download it and read it carefully at least three weeks

before your exam.

Refer to the following links:
http://www.gbci.org/main-nav/professional-credentials/resources/candidate-handbooks.aspx

http://www.usgbc.org/resources/leed-v4-ap-bdc-candidate-handbook

Chapter Three

Frequently Asked Questions (FAQ) and Other Useful Resources

The following are tips on how to pass the LEED exam on the first try with only one week of preparation. I also include my responses to several readers' questions. Hopefully they may help you.

I. **I found the reference guide way too tedious. Can I only read your books and just refer to the USGBC reference guide (if one is available for the exam I am taking) when needed?**

   Response: Yes. That is one way to study.

II. **Is one week really enough for me to prepare for the exam while I am working?**
   Response: Yes, if you can put in 40 to 60 hours during the week, study hard and you can pass the exam. This exam is similar to a

history or political science exam; you need to MEMORIZE the information. If you take too long, you will probably forget the information by the time you take the test.

In my book, I give you tips on how to MEMORIZE the information, and I have already highlighted/underlined the most important information that you definitely have to MEMORIZE to pass the exam. It is my goal to use this book to help you to pass the LEED exam with the minimum time and effort. I want to make your life easier.

III. Would you say that if I buy your LEED Exam Guide Series books, I could pass the exam using no other study materials? The books sold on the USGBC website run in the hundreds of dollars, so I would be quite happy if I could buy your book and just use that.

Response: First of all, there are readers who have passed the LEED Exam by reading only my books in the LEED Exam Guides series (www.GreenExamEducation.com). My goal is to write at least one book for each of the LEED exams, and my books stand alone to prepare people for one specific LEED exam.

Secondly, people learn in many different ways. That is why I have added some new advice below for people who learn better by doing practice tests.

If you do the following things, you have a very good chance of passing the LEED exam (NOT a guarantee, nobody can guarantee you will pass):

a. If you study, understand and MEMORIZE all of the information in my books, *LEED v4 BD &C Exam Guide* and *LEED v4 BD&C Mock Exam*, and do NOT panic when you run into problems you are not familiar with, and use the guess strategy in my books, then you have a very good chance of passing the exam.

You need to UNDERSTAND and MEMORIZE the information in the books and score almost a perfect score on the mock exam in my book. This book will give you the BULK of the most CURRENT information that you need for the specific LEED exam you are taking. You HAVE to know the information in my book in order to pass the exam.

b. If you have not done any LEED projects before, I suggest you also go to the USGBC website and download the latest LEED credit templates for the LEED rating system related to the LEED exam you are taking. Read the templates and become familiar with them. This is important. Refer to the following link:

http://www.usgbc.org/leed#rating

The LEED exam is NOT an easy exam, but anyone with a 7th grade education should be able to study and pass the LEED exam if he prepares correctly.

If you have extra time and money, the other books I would recommend is *LEED GA Mock Exams (LEED v4)* and the USGBC reference guide, the official book for the LEED exam. I know some people who did not even read the reference guide from cover to cover when they took the exam. They just studied the information in my books, and only referred to the reference guide to look up a few things, and they passed on the first try. Some of my readers have even passed WITHOUT reading the USGBC reference guide AT ALL.

IV. I am preparing for the LEED exam. Do I need to read the 2" thick reference?

Response: See answer above.

V. For LEED v4, will the total number of points be more than 110 in total if a project gets all of the extra credits and all of the standard credits?

Response: No. For LEED v4, there are 100

base points and 10 possible bonus points. There are many ways to get bonus points (extra credits or exemplary performance), but you can have a maximum number of 6 ID bonus points and 4 Regional Priority bonus points. So, the maximum points for ANY project will be 110.

On another note, the older versions of LEED rating systems all have less than 110 possible points except LEED for **Home**, which has 136 possible points.

VI. **For the exam, do I need to know the project phase in which a specific prerequisite/credit takes place? (i.e., pre-design, schematic design, etc.)**

Response: The information on the project phase (NOT LEED submittal phase) for each prerequisite/credit is NOT mentioned in the USGBC reference guide, but it is covered in the USGBC workshops. If it is important enough for the USGBC workshops to cover, then it may show up on the actual LEED exam.

Most, if not all, other third party books completely miss this important information. I cover it for each prerequisite/credit in my book for the LEED exam because I think it is very important.

Some people THINK that the LEED exam ONLY tests information covered by the USGBC reference guide. They are wrong.

The LEED exam does test information NOT covered by the USGBC reference guide at all. This may include the process of LEED submittal and project team coordination, etc.

I would MEMORIZE this information if I were you, because it may show up on the LEED exam. Besides, this information is not hard to memorize once you understand it, and you need to know it to do actual LEED submittal work anyway.

VII. Are you writing new versions of books for the new LEED exams? What new books are you writing?

Response: Yes, I am working on other books in the LEED Exam Guide series. I will be writing one book for each of the LEED exam. See GreenExamEducation.com for more information.

VIII. Important documents that you need to download for free, become familiar with and memorize:

Note: GBCI and USGBC change the links to their document every now and then, so, by the time you read this book, they may have changed some of the following links. You can simply go to their main website, search for the document with its name, and should be able to find the most current link. You can use the same technique to search for documents by other organizations.

The main website for the GBCI is:
http://www.gbci.org/

The main website for the USGBC is:
http://www.usgbc.org/

a. Every LEED exam **always tests** Credit Interpretation Request (CIR). Download the guidelines for CIR customers, read and memorize it:
http://www.gbci.org/Certification/Resources/cirs.aspx

Every LEED exam **always tests** project team coordination. Download *Sustainable Building Technical Manual: Part II,* by Anthony Bernheim and William Reed (1996), read and memorize it:
http://www.gbci.org/Files/References/Sustai

nable-Building-Technical-Manual-Part-II.pdf

b. Project registration application and LEED certification process: http://www.usgbc.org/certification

c. LEED Online: https://leedonline.usgbc.org/Login.aspx

IX. Important documents that you need to download for <u>free</u>, and become <u>familiar</u> with:

a. *LEED for Operations and Maintenance Reference Guide-Introduction* (U.S. Green Building Council, 2013): http://www.usgbc.org/sites/all/assets/section/files/v4-guide-excerpts/Excerpt_v4_OM.pdf

b. *LEED for Operations and Maintenance Reference Guide-Glossary* (U.S. Green Building Council, 2008): http://www.gbci.org/Files/References/LEED-for-Operations-and-Maintenance-Reference-Guide-Glossary.pdf

c. *LEED for Homes Rating System* (U.S. Green Building Council, 2008): http://www.gbci.org/Files/References/LEED-for-Homes-Rating-System.pdf

Pay special attention to the list of **abbreviations and acronyms** on pages 105–106 and the helpful **glossary of terms** on pages 107–114.

d. *Cost of Green Revisited,* by Davis Langdon (2007):
http://www.gbci.org/Files/References/Cost-of-Green-Revisited.pdf

e. *The Treatment by LEED® of the Environmental Impact of HVAC Refrigerants (*LEED Technical and Scientific Advisory Committee, 2004):
http://www.gbci.org/Files/References/The-Treatment-by-LEED-of-the-Environmental-Impact-of-HVAC-Refrigerants.pdf

f. *Guidance on Innovation and Design (ID) Credits* (US Green Building Council, 2004):
http://www.gbci.org/Files/References/Guidance-on-Innovation-and-Design-Credits.pdf

X. Do I need to take many practice questions to prepare for a LEED exam?

Response: There is NO absolutely correct answer to this question. People learn in many different ways. Personally, I am NOT crazy about doing many practice questions. Consider if you do 700 practice questions, not only must you read them all, but each question has at least 4 choices. That totals to at least 2,800 choices, which is a great deal of reading. I have seen some third-party materials that have 1,200 practice questions. That will require even MORE time to go over the materials.

I prefer to spend most of my time reading, digesting, and really understanding the fundamental materials, and MEMORIZE them naturally by rereading the materials multiple times. This is because the fundamental materials for ANY exam will NOT change, and the scope of the exam will NOT change for the same main version of the test (until the exam moves to the next advanced version). However, there are many ways to ask you questions.

If you have a limited amount of time for preparation, it is more efficient for you to focus on the fundamental materials and actually <u>master</u> the knowledge that GBCI wants you to learn. If you can do that, then no matter how GBCI changes the exam format or how GBCI asks the questions, you will do fine in the exam.

Strategy 101 for the LEED AP BD+C Exam is that you must recognize that you have only a limited amount of time to prepare for the exam. Therefore, you must concentrate on the most important contents of the LEED AP BD+C Exam.

The key to passing the LEED AP BD+C Exam, or any other exam, is to know the scope of the exam, and not to read too many books. Select one or two helpful books and focus on them. You must understand the content and memorize it. For your convenience, I have underlined the fundamental information that I think is very important. You definitely need to memorize all the information that I have underlined. You should try to understand the content first, and then memorize the content of the book by rereading it. This is a much better way than "mechanical" memory without understanding.

Most people fail the exam NOT because they are unable to answer the few "advanced" questions on the exam, but because they have read the information but can NOT recall it on the day of the exam. They spend too much time preparing for the exam, drag the preparation process on too long, seek too much information, go to too many Web sites, do too many practice questions and too many mock exams (one or two sets of mock exams are probably sufficient), and spread themselves too thin. They end up missing out on the most important information of the LEED exam, and they will fail.

To me, Memorization and understanding work hand-in-hand. Understanding always comes first. If you really understand something, then Memorization is easy.

For example, I'll read a book's first chapter very slowly but make sure I <u>really</u> understand everything in it, no matter how long it takes. I do NOT care if others are faster readers than I.

Then, I reread the first chapter again. This time, the reading is so much easier, and I can read it much faster. Then I try to retell the contents, focusing on substance, not the format or any particular order of things. This is a very good way for me to understand and digest the material, while <u>absorbing</u> and <u>memorizing</u> the content.

I then repeat the same procedure for each chapter, and then reread the book until I take the exam. This achieves two purposes:

a. I keep reinforcing the important materials that I already have memorized and fight against the human brain's natural tendency to forget things.

b. I also understand the content of the book much better by reading it multiple times.

If I were to attempt to memorize something without understanding it first, it would be very difficult for me to do so. Even if I were to memorize it, I would likely forget it quickly.

Appendixes

I. Default occupancy factors

Occupancy	Gross sf per occupant	
	Transient Occupant	FTE
Educational, Daycare	630	105
Educational, K–12	1,300	140
Educational, Postsecondary	2,100	150
Grocery store	550	115
Hotel	1,500	700
Laboratory or R&D	400	0
Office, Medical	225	330
Office, General	250	0
Retail, General	550	130
Retail or Service (auto, financial, etc.)	600	130
Restaurant	435	95
Warehouse, Distribution	2,500	0
Warehouse, Storage	20,000	0

Note: This table is for projects (like CS) where the final occupant count is not available. If your project's occupancy factors are not listed above, you can use a comparable building to show the average gross sf per occupant for your building's use.

II. Official reference materials listed by the GBCI

For Exam Part 1: LEED® Green Associate™ Exam:

U.S. Green Building Council. *Green Building and LEED Core Concepts Guide*. 3rd Edition. U.S. Green Building Council, 2011. Print and Digital versions available.
http://www.usgbc.org/resources/leed-core-concepts-guide

U.S. Green Building Council. *Introductory and Overview Sections. LEED Building Design + Construction Reference Guide*. v4 Edition. U.S. Green Building Council, 2013.
Note: the introductory and overview sections are available to download for FREE, separately from purchasing the full

reference guide.
http://www.usgbc.org/resources/leed-reference-guide-building-design-and-construction.

U.S. Green Building Council. *LEED v4 Impact Category and Point Allocation Process Overview*. U.S. Green Building Council, 2013.
http://www.usgbc.org/resources/leed-v4-impact-category-and-point-allocation-process-overview

U.S. Green Building Council. *LEED v4 User Guide*. U.S. Green Building Council, 2013.
http://www.usgbc.org/resources/leed-v4-user-guide

U.S. Green Building Council. *Guide to LEED Certification: Commercia*l. U.S. Green Building Council, 2014.
http://www.usgbc.org/resources/guide-leed-certification-commerical

"LEED Certification Fees." U.S. Green Building Council, 2014.
http://www.usgbc.org/cert-guide/fees

"Rating System Selection Guidance." U.S. Green Building Council, 2014.

http://www.usgbc.org/resources/rating-system-selection-guidance

Exam Part 2: LEED® AP BD+C Specialty Exam

U.S. Green Building Council. *LEED Building Design and Construction Reference Guide*. v4 Edition. U.S. Green Building Council, 2013.
http://www.usgbc.org/resources/leed-reference-guide-building-design-and-construction

"Green building incentive strategies." U. S. Green Building Council, 2014.
http://www.usgbc.org/advocacy/priorities/incentives-financing

U.S. Green Building Council. *Guide to LEED Certification: Commercial*. U.S. Green Building Council, 2014.
http://www.usgbc.org/resources/guide-leed-certification-commerical

U.S. Green Building Council. *Foundations of LEED*. U.S. Green Building Council, 2009.
http://www.usgbc.org/resources/foundations-leed

U.S. Green Building Council. *LEED v4 for Building Design and Construction Checklist*. U.S. Green Building Council, 2013.
http://www.usgbc.org/resources/leed-v4-building-design-and-construction-checklist

"LEED Addenda (Corrections + Interpretations)." U. S. Green Building Council, 2014.
http://www.usgbc.org/help-topic/addenda-(corrections-+-interpretations)

"LEED Online: Register a project." U.S. Green Building Council, 2014.
https://www.usgbc.org/leedonline.new/

"LEED Certification Fees." U.S. Green Building Council, 2014.
http://www.usgbc.org/cert-guide/fees

"Rating System Selection Guidance." U.S. Green Building Council, 2014.
http://www.usgbc.org/cert-guide/fees

III. Important resources and further study materials you can download for <u>free</u>

Energy Performance of LEED® for New Construction Buildings: Final Report, by Cathy Turner and Mark Frankel (2008):
http://www.gbci.org/Files/References/Energy-Performance-of-LEED-for-New-Construction-Buildings-Final-Report.pdf

Foundations of the Leadership in Energy and Environmental Design Environmental Rating System: A Tool for Market Transformation (LEED Steering Committee, 2006):
http://www.gbci.org/Files/References/Foundations-of-the-Leadership-in-Energy-and-Environmental-Design-Environmental-Rating-System-A-Tool-for-Market-Transformation.pdf

AIA Integrated Project Delivery: A Guide (www.aia.org):
http://www.aia.org/contractdocs/AIAS077630

Review of ANSI/ASHRAE Standard 62.1-2004: Ventilation for Acceptable Indoor Air Quality, by Brian Kareis:

http://www.workplace-hygiene.com/articles/ANSI-ASHRAE-3.html

Best Practices of ISO - 14021: Self-Declared Environmental Claims, by Kun-Mo Lee and Haruo Uehara (2003): http://books.google.be/books/about/Best_practices_of_ISO_14021.html?hl=nl&id=e2eCAAAACAAJ

Bureau of Labor Statistics (www.bls.gov)

International Code Council (www.iccsafe.org)

Americans with Disabilities Act (ADA): Standards for Accessible Design (www.ada.gov): http://www.ada.gov/stdspdf.htm

GSA Facilities Standards (General Services Administration, Latest Edition): *http://www.gsa.gov/portal/content/104821*

Guide to Purchasing Green Power (Environmental Protection Agency, 2004): http://www.gbci.org/Files/References/G

uide-to-Purchasing-Green-Power.pdf

USGBC Definitions: https://www.usgbc.org/ShowFile.aspx?DocumentID=5744

IV. Annotated bibliography

Chen, Gang. *LEED v4 Green Associate Exam Guide (LEED GA): Comprehensive Study Materials, Sample Questions, Mock Exam, Green Building LEED Certification, and Sustainability*, Book 2, LEED Exam Guide series, ArchiteG.com. Latest Edition ArchiteG, Inc. This is a very comprehensive and concise book on the LEED Green Associate Exam. Some readers have passed the LEED Green Associate Exam by studying this book for 10 hours in total.

Chen, Gang. *LEED GA MOCK EXAMS (LEED v4): Questions, Answers, and Explanations: A Must-Have for the LEED Green Associate Exam, Green Building LEED Certification, and Sustainability*. Latest Edition. ArchiteG, Inc. This is a companion to LEED Green Associate Exam Guide. It includes 200 questions, answers, and explanation, and is very close to the real LEED Green Associate Exam.

V. Valuable Web sites and links

a. The Official Websites for the U.S. Green Building Council (USGBC):
http://www.usgbc.org/
http://www.Greenbuild365.org

Pay special attention to the purpose of <u>LEED Online, LEED project registration, LEED certification content, LEED reference guide introductions, LEED rating systems, and checklists</u>.

You can download or purchase the following useful documents from the USGBC or GBCI website:

Latest and official LEED exam candidate handbooks including an exam content outline and sample questions:
http://www.usgbc.org/resources/list/credentialing-resources

LEED Reference Guides:
http://www.usgbc.org/leed/v4

LEED Rating System Selection:
http://www.usgbc.org/certification

Read the document above <u>at least three times</u>, because it is VERY important, and tells you which LEED system to use.

Various versions of LEED Green Building Rating Systems and Project Checklist:
http://www.usgbc.org/leed/v4

USGBC issue LEED Addenda for various LEED Green Building Rating **Systems** and **reference guides** on a quarterly basis. **Make sure you download the latest LEED Addenda** related to your exam and read them at least three times. See link below for detailed information:
http://www.usgbc.org/addenda

b. Natural Resources Defense Council:
http://www.nrdc.org/

c. Environmental Construction + Design - Green Book (Offers print magazine and on-line environmental products and services resources guide):
http://www.edcmag.com/greenbook

d. Cool Roof Rating Council website: http://www.coolroofs.org

VI. Important Items Covered by the Second Edition of *Green Building and LEED Core Concepts Guide*

Starting on December 1, 2011, GBCI will begin to draw LEED Green Associate Exam questions from the second edition of *Green Building and LEED Core Concepts Guide*. The following are some "new" and important items covered by this edition:

adaptive reuse: Designing and constructing a building to accommodate a future use that is different from its original use.

biomimicry: Learning from nature and designing systems using principles that have been tested in nature for millions of years.

carbon overlay: LEED credit weighting based on each credit's impact on reducing carbon footprint.

charrettes: Intensive (design) workshops.

cradle to cradle: A method where materials are used in a closed system and generate no waste.

cradle to grave: A process that examines materials from their point of extraction to disposal.

closed system: There is no "away." Everything goes somewhere within the system, the waste generated by a process becomes the "food" of another process. Nature is a closed system.

embodied energy: The total energy consumed by extracting, harvesting, manufacturing, transporting, installing, and using a material through its entire life cycle.

ENERGY STAR's Portfolio Manager: An online management tool for tracking and evaluating water and energy use. An ENERGY STAR Portfolio Manager score of 50 means a building is at national average energy use level for its category. A score higher than 50 means a building is more energy efficient than the national average energy use level for its category. The higher the score, the better.

evapotranspiration: Loss of water due to evaporation.

externalities: Benefits or costs that are NOT part of a transaction.

feedback loop: Information flows within a system that allows the system to adjust itself. A thermostat or melting snow is an example of negative feedback loop. Population growth, heat island effect, or climate change is a positive feedback loop. Positive feedback loop can create chaos in a system.

International Green Construction Code (IGCC): A national model green building code published by International Code Council (ICC).

integrated process: Emphasizes communications and interactions among stakeholders throughout the life of a project. Integrated process is a holistic decision making process based on systems thinking and life cycle approach.

interative process: A repetitive and circular process that helps a team to define goals and check ideas against these goals.

Integrated Pest Management (IPM): A sustainable approach to pest management.

LEED interpretations: Precedent-setting (project credit interpretation) rulings. A project team can opt into the LEED interpretation process when submitting an inquiry to GBCI.

leverage points: Places where a small interventions can generate big changes.

life cycle approach: Looking at a product or building through its entire life cycle.

life cycle assessment (LCA): Use life cycle thinking in environmental issues.

life cycle costing: Looking at the cost of purchasing and operating a building or product, and the relative savings.

low impact development (LID): A land development approach mimicking natural systems and managing storm water as close to the source as possible.

"Net-Zero": A project, which doesn't use any more resources than what it can produce. Similar concepts include carbon neutrality and water balance.

negative feedback loop: A signal for the system to stop changes when a response is not needed anymore.

open system: Resources are brought from the outside, consumed, and then disposed of as waste to the outside.

permaculture: Designing human habitats and agriculture systems based on models and relationships found in nature.

positive feedback loop: A stimulus causes an effect and encourages the loop to produce more of this effect.

Prius effect: Provides real time feedback of energy use so that users can adjust behaviors to save energy.

Project CIRs: LEED credit interpretation rulings for specific project circumstances.

retrocommissioning: A building tune-up that restores efficiency and improves performance.

regenerative: Regenerative buildings and communities evolve with living systems and help to renew resources and life. Regenerative projects generate electricity and sell the excess back to the grid, as well as return water to nature, which is cleaner than it was before use.

systems thinking: In a system, each component affects many other components. They are all related to each other.

Wingspread Principles on the US Response to Global Warming: A set of principles signed by organizations and individuals to express their commitment to address global warming. It calls for 60% to 80% reduction of greenhouse gas emission by midcentury (based on 1990 levels).

Back page promotion

You may be interested in some other books written by Gang Chen:

A. **ARE Mock Exam series. See following link:**
http://www.GreenExamEducation.com

B. **LEED Exam Guides series. See following link:**
http://www.GreenExamEducation.com

C. *Building Construction: Project Management, Construction Administration, Drawings, Specs, Detailing Tips, Schedules, Checklists, and Secrets Others Don't Tell You (Architectural Practice Simplified, 2nd edition)*
http://www.ArchiteG.com

D. *Planting Design Illustrated*
http://www.GreenExamEducation.com

ARE Mock Exam Series

Published ARE & California Supplemental Exam (CSE) books:

Programming, Planning & Practice ARE Mock Exam (PPP of Architect Registration Exam): ARE Overview, Exam Prep Tips, Multiple-Choice Questions and Graphic Vignettes, Solutions and Explanations
ISBN-13: 9781612650067

Site Planning & Design ARE Mock Exam (SPD of Architect Registration Exam): ARE Overview, Exam Prep Tips, Multiple-Choice Questions and Graphic Vignettes, Solutions and Explanations
ISBN-13: 9781612650111

Building Design and Construction Systems (BDCS) ARE Mock Exam (Architect Registration Exam): ARE Overview, Exam Prep Tips, Multiple-Choice Questions and Graphic Vignettes, Solutions and Explanations
ISBN-13: 9781612650029

Schematic Design (SD) ARE Mock Exam (Architect Registration Exam): ARE Overview, Exam Prep Tips, Graphic Vignettes, Solutions and Explanations
ISBN-13: 9781612650050

Structural Systems ARE Mock Exam (SS of Architect Registration Exam): ARE Overview, Exam Prep Tips, Multiple-Choice Questions and Graphic Vignettes, Solutions and Explanations
ISBN-13: 9781612650012

Building Systems (BS) ARE Mock Exam (Architect Registration Exam): ARE Overview, Exam Prep Tips, Multiple-Choice Questions and Graphic Vignettes, Solutions and Explanations
ISBN-13: 9781612650036

Construction Documents and Service (CDS) Are Mock Exam (Architect Registration Exam): ARE Overview, Exam Prep Tips, Multiple-Choice Questions and Graphic Vignettes, Solutions and Explanations
ISBN-13: 9781612650005

Mock California Supplemental Exam (CSE of Architect Registration Exam): CSE Overview, Exam Prep Tips, General Section and Project Scenario Section, Questions, Solutions and Explanations
ISBN: 9781612650159

See the following link for the latest information on all our books:
http://www.**GreenExamEducation**.com

Check out FREE tips and info for all ARE Exams at **GeeForum**.com, you can post jpeg files of your vignettes or your questions for other users' review.

LEED Exam Guides Series: Comprehensive Study Materials, Sample Questions, Mock Exam, Building LEED Certification and Going Green

LEED (Leadership in Energy and Environmental Design) is the most important trend of development, and it is revolutionizing the construction industry. It has gained tremendous momentum and has a profound impact on our environment.

From LEED Exam Guides series, you will learn how to

1. Pass the LEED Green Associate Exam and various LEED AP + exams (each book will help you with a specific LEED exam).
2. Register and certify a building for LEED certification.
3. Understand the intent for each LEED prerequisite and credit.
4. Calculate points for a LEED credit.
5. Identify the responsible party for each prerequisite and credit.
6. Earn extra credit (exemplary performance) for LEED.
7. Implement the local codes and building standards for prerequisites and credit.
8. Receive points for categories not yet clearly defined by USGBC.

   There is currently NO official GBCI book on the LEED Green Associate Exam, and most of the existing books on LEED and LEED AP are too expensive and too complicated to be practical and helpful. The LEED Exam Guides series fill in the blanks, demystify LEED, and uncover the tips, codes, and jargon for LEED as well as the true meaning of "going green." They will set up a solid foundation and fundamental framework of LEED for you. Each book in the LEED Exam Guides series covers every aspect of one or more specific LEED rating system(s) in plain and concise language and makes this information understandable to all people.

These books are small and easy to carry around. You can read them whenever you have a few extra minutes. They are indispensable books for all people—administrators; developers; contractors; architects; landscape architects; civil, mechanical, electrical, and plumbing engineers; interns; drafters; designers; and other design professionals.

Why is the LEED Exam Guides series needed?

A number of books are available that you can use to prepare for the LEED Exams:

1. *USGBC Reference Guides.* You need to select the correct version of the *Reference*

Guide for your exam.

The *USGBC Reference Guides* are comprehensive, and they give too much information. For example, *The LEED v4 Reference Guide for Green Building Design and Construction (BD&C)* has about 817 oversized pages. Many of the calculations in the books are too detailed for the exam. They are also expensive (approximately $200 each, so most people may not buy them for their personal use, but instead, will seek to share an office copy).

It is good to read a reference guide from cover to cover if you have the time. The problem is not too many people have time to read the whole reference guide. Even if you do read the whole guide, you may not remember the important issues to pass the LEED exam. You need to reread the material several times before you can remember much of it.

Reading the reference guide from cover to cover without a guidebook is a difficult and inefficient way of preparing for the LEED AP Exam, because you do NOT know what USGBC and GBCI are looking for in the exam.

2. The USGBC workshops and related handouts are concise, but they do not cover extra

credits (exemplary performance). The workshops are expensive, costing approximately $450 each.

3. Various books published by a third party are available online. However, most of them are not very helpful.

   There are many books on LEED, but not all are useful.

   LEED Exam Guides series will fill in the blanks and become a valuable, reliable source:

a. They will give you more information for your money. Each of the books in the LEED Exam Guides series has more information than the related USGBC workshops.

b. They are exam-oriented and more effective than the USGBC reference guides.

c. They are better than most, if not all, of the other third-party books. They give you comprehensive study materials, sample questions and answers, mock exams and answers, and critical information on building LEED certification and going green. Other third-party books only give you a fraction of the information.

d. They are comprehensive yet concise. They are small and easy to carry around. You can read them whenever you have a few extra minutes.

e. They are great timesavers. I have highlighted the important information that you need to understand and MEMORIZE. I also make some acronyms and short sentences to help you easily remember the credit names.

It should take you about 1 or 2 weeks of full-time study to pass each of the LEED exams. I have met people who have spent 40 hours to study and passed the exams.

You can find sample texts and other information about the LEED Exam Guide, and check out FREE tips on the easiest way to pass the LEED exams and info for all LEED Exams and ARE Exams at **GeeForum.com**, you can post your questions for other users' review.

What others are saying about *LEED Green Associate Exam Guide*…

"Finally! A comprehensive study tool for LEED Green Associate Prep!"
"I took the one-day Green LEED Green Associate course and walked away with a power point binder printed in very small print—which was missing MUCH of the required information (although I didn't know it at the time). I studied my little heart out and

took the test, only to fail it by 1 point. Turns out I did NOT study all the material I needed to in order to pass the test. I found this book, read it, marked it up, retook the test, and passed it with a 95%. Look, we all know the LEED Green Associate Exam is new and the resources for study are VERY limited. This one's the VERY best out there right now. I highly recommend it."
—Consultant VA

"Complete overview for the LEED Green Associate exam"
"I studied this book for about three days and passed the exam … if you are truly interested in learning about the LEED system and green building design, this is a great place to start."
—K.A. Evans

"Very effective study guide"
"I purchased both this study guide and Mr. Chen's LEED GA Mock Exams book and found them to be excellent tools for preparing for the LEED Green Associate Exam. While Mr. Chen's LEED Green Associate Exam Guide is not perfect (in that it's not the most user-friendly presentation of the material), it was very effective in at least presenting most, if not all, of the topics that the exam touched upon. While I wouldn't necessarily recommend my abbreviated strategy for preparing for the exam, the following worked for me: I read through the exam guide a couple of times (but not word for word), took the mock exam and referenced the guide for explanations for any wrong answers, did the same for

the two mock exams in Mr. Chen's LEED GA Mock Exams book, flipped through the documents that Mr. Chen recommends, and took two other web-based mock exams that I purchased on eBay. Literally after ten hours of preparation time, I took the actual exam and passed with a 189, thanks in large part to Mr. Chen's books. If I decide to take one of the LEED AP exams in the future, I will definitely be picking up more of Mr. Chen's study materials."
—shwee "shwee"

"Only study guide needed to pass on your first try"
"I don't write reviews, but I'm compelled to for this purchase. This was the only book I read and studied to prepare for the LEED Green Associate exam, and passed with ease on the first try today. I was over prepared for the exam by using this study guide, which is what I wanted on exam day. I bought the book, read it three times, learned a lot of good information, saved valuable time, and passed on the first try. By the way, I'm not a good test taker. I don't agree with any of the negative reviews that are posted... I'm glad I ignored those when I made the purchase and went with the majority. THIS PRODUCT DELIVERED THE RESULTS, CASE CLOSED. I'll be buying his *LEED AP BD&C Exam Guide* to prepare for the specialty exam. Thank you Mr. Gang Chen!!!"
—Lobo

"I just finished taking the LEED Green Associate Exam and, thankfully, I passed it on the first try by

using this book as my primary study guide...I particularly liked the way the author organized the information within it."
—**Lewis Colon**

Note: Other books in the **LEED Exam Guides series** are in the process of being produced. At least **One book will eventually be produced for each of the LEED exams.** The series include:

LEED v4 Green Associate Exam Guide (LEED GA): *Comprehensive Study Materials, Sample Questions, Mock Exam, Green Building LEED Certification, and Sustainability*, LEED Exam Guide series, ArchiteG.com. Latest Edition.

LEED GA MOCK EXAMS (LEED v4): *Questions, Answers, and Explanations: A Must-Have for the LEED Green Associate Exam, Green Building LEED Certification, and Sustainability*, LEED Exam Guide series, ArchiteG.com. Latest Edition

LEED v4 BD&C EXAM GUIDE: *A Must-Have for the LEED AP BD+C Exam: Comprehensive Study Materials, Sample Questions, Mock Exam, Green Building Design and Construction, LEED Certification, and Sustainability*, LEED Exam Guide series, ArchiteG.com. Latest Edition.

LEED v4 BD&C MOCK EXAMS: *Questions, Answers, and Explanations: A Must-Have for the LEED AP BD+C Exam, Green Building LEED*

Certification, and Sustainability, LEED Exam Guide series, ArchiteG.com. Latest Edition.

LEED AP Exam Guide: *Study Materials, Sample Questions, Mock Exam, Building LEED Certification, and Going Green*, LEED Exam Guides series, LEEDSeries.com. Latest Edition.

LEED ID&C EXAM GUIDE: *A Must-Have for the LEED AP ID+C Exam: Comprehensive Study Materials, Sample Questions, Mock Exam, Green Interior Design and Construction, LEED Certification, and Sustainability*, LEED Exam Guide series, ArchiteG.com. Latest Edition.

LEED O&M MOCK EXAMS: *Questions, Answers, and Explanations: A Must-Have for the LEED O&M Exam, Green Building LEED Certification, and Sustainability*, LEED Exam Guide series, ArchiteG.com. Latest Edition.

LEED O&M EXAM GUIDE: *A Must-Have for the LEED AP O+M Exam: Comprehensive Study Materials, Sample Questions, Mock Exam, Green Building Operations and Maintenance, LEED Certification, and Sustainability*, LEED Exam Guide series, ArchiteG.com. Latest Edition.

LEED HOMES EXAM GUIDE: *A Must-Have for the LEED AP Homes Exam: Comprehensive Study Materials, Sample Questions, Mock Exam, Green Building LEED Certification, and Sustainability*,

LEED Exam Guide series, ArchiteG.com. Latest Edition.

LEED ND EXAM GUIDE: *A Must-Have for the LEED AP Neighborhood Development Exam: Comprehensive Study Materials, Sample Questions, Mock Exam, Green Building LEED Certification, and Sustainability*, LEED Exam Guide series, ArchiteG.com. Latest Edition.

How to order these books:
You can order the books listed above at:
http://www.GreenExamEducation.com

Check out FREE tips and info for all LEED Exams at **GeeForum**.com, you can post your questions for other users' review.

Building Construction

Project Management, Construction Administration, Drawings, Specs, Detailing Tips, Schedules, Checklists, and Secrets Others Don't Tell You
(Architectural Practice Simplified, 2nd edition)

Learn the Tips, Become One of Those Who Know Building Construction and Architectural Practice, and Thrive!

For architectural practice and building design and construction industry, there are two kinds of people: those who know, and those who don't. The tips of building design and construction and project management have been undercover—until now.

Most of the existing books on building construction and architectural practice are too expensive, too complicated, and too long to be practical and helpful. This book simplifies the process to make it easier to understand and uncovers the tips of building design and construction and project management. It sets up a solid foundation and fundamental framework for this field. It covers every aspect of building construction and architectural practice in plain and concise language and introduces it to all people. Through practical case studies, it demonstrates the efficient and proper ways to handle various issues and problems in architectural practice and building design and construction industry.

It is for ordinary people and aspiring young architects as well as seasoned professionals in the construction industry. For ordinary people, it uncovers the tips of building construction; for aspiring architects, it works as a construction industry survival guide and a guidebook to shorten the process in mastering architectural practice and climbing up the professional ladder; for seasoned architects, it has many checklists to refresh their memory. It is an indispensable reference book for ordinary people, architectural students, interns, drafters, designers, seasoned architects, engineers, construction administrators, superintendents, construction managers, contractors, and developers.

You will learn:
1. How to develop your business and work with your client.
2. The entire process of building design and construction, including programming, entitlement, schematic design, design development, construction documents, bidding, and construction administration.
3. How to coordinate with governing agencies, including a county's health department and a city's planning, building, fire, public works departments, etc.
4. How to coordinate with your consultants, including soils, civil, structural, electrical, mechanical, plumbing engineers, landscape architects, etc.

5. How to create and use your own checklists to do quality control of your construction documents.
6. How to use various logs (i.e., RFI log, submittal log, field visit log, etc.) and lists (contact list, document control list, distribution list, etc.) to organize and simplify your work.
7. How to respond to RFI, issue CCDs, review change orders, submittals, etc.
8. How to make your architectural practice a profitable and successful business.

Planting Design Illustrated
A Must-Have for Landscape Architecture: A Holistic Garden Design Guide with Architectural and Horticultural Insight, and Ideas from Famous Gardens in Major Civilizations

One of the most significant books on landscaping!

This is one of the most comprehensive books on planting design. It fills in the blanks of the field and introduces poetry, painting, and symbolism into planting design. It covers in detail the two major systems of planting design: formal planting design and naturalistic planting design. It has numerous line drawings and photos to illustrate the planting design concepts and principles. Through in-depth discussions of historical precedents and practical case studies, it uncovers the fundamental design principles and concepts, as well as the underpinning philosophy for planting design. It is an indispensable reference book for landscape architecture students, designers, architects, urban planners, and ordinary garden lovers.

What Others Are Saying About *Planting Design Illustrated* ...

"I found this book to be absolutely fascinating. You will need to concentrate while reading it, but the effort will be well worth your time."
—**Bobbie Schwartz, former president of APLD (Association of Professional Landscape Designers) and author of** *The Design Puzzle: Putting the Pieces Together*.

"This is a book that you have to read, and it is more than well worth your time. Gang Chen takes you well beyond what you will learn in other books about basic principles like color, texture, and mass."
—**Jane Berger, editor & publisher of gardendesignonline**

"As a longtime consumer of gardening books, I am impressed with Gang Chen's inclusion of new information on planting design theory for Chinese and Japanese gardens. Many gardening books discuss the beauty of Japanese gardens, and a few discuss the unique charms of Chinese gardens, but this one explains how Japanese and Chinese history, as well as geography and artistic traditions, bear on the development of each country's style. The material on traditional Western garden planting is thorough and inspiring, too. *Planting Design Illustrated* definitely rewards repeated reading and study. Any garden designer will read it with profit."
—**Jan Whitner, editor of the** *Washington Park Arboretum Bulletin*

"Enhanced with an annotated bibliography and informative appendices, *Planting Design Illustrated* offers an especially "reader friendly" and practical guide that makes it a very strongly recommended addition to personal, professional, academic, and community library gardening & landscaping reference collection and supplemental reading list."
—Midwest Book Review

"Where to start? *Planting Design Illustrated* is, above all, fascinating and refreshing! Not something the lay reader encounters every day, the book presents an unlikely topic in an easily digestible, easy-to-follow way. It is superbly organized with a comprehensive table of contents, bibliography, and appendices. The writing, though expertly informative, maintains its accessibility throughout and is a joy to read. The detailed and beautiful illustrations expanding on the concepts presented were my favorite portion. One of the finest books I've encountered in this contest in the past 5 years."
—Writer's Digest 16th Annual International Self-Published Book Awards Judge's Commentary

"The work in my view has incredible application to planting design generally and a system approach to what is a very difficult subject to teach, at least in my experience. Also featured is a very beautiful philosophy of garden design principles bordering poetry. It's my strong conviction that this work needs to see the light of day by being published for the use of professionals, students & garden enthusiasts."

—Donald C. Brinkerhoff, FASLA, chairman and CEO of Lifescapes International, Inc.

Index

40/60 rule, 42, 110, 131
Albedo, 36, 50, 119
American Council for an Energy Efficient Economy (ACEEE), 108, 109
ammonia (NH3), 55
ANSI, 136
ASHRAE, 87, 165
association factors, 183
Basic Services, 116
blackwater, 33, 57, 104, 121, 124
BOD, 70, 145
BUG, 97, 177
CARB, 149
Carbon Trust, 87, 165
CFC, 32, 39, 50, 55, 107, 119, 123
CFCs, 32, 39, 54, 78, 103, 108, 119, 120, 122, 154
CGP, 138
CI, 137
CIR, 56, 63, 64, 65, 132, 134, 135, 193
CIRs, 47, 56, 65, 116, 124
Commissioning, 73, 84, 88, 96, 97, 98, 99, 160, 165, 176, 178, 179, 180
Cradle-to-cradle, 50, 118
CRS, 79, 156
CSI MasterFormat™, 80, 81, 157, 158
Energy Policy Act (EPAct), 34, 104
EPA, 71, 146
ESC, 92, 138, 171
FAR, 33, 45, 103, 114
FTE, 201
GBCI, 15, 16, 65, 66, 79, 136, 156, 181, 185
graywater, 33, 40, 49, 57, 103, 109, 118, 124
green power, 36, 58, 119
Green Rater, 64, 133, 134
Green-e, 36, 39, 51, 105, 108

GWP, 48, 54, 55, 116, 121, 122, 123
Halon, 40, 109
HCFCs, 78, 154
Heat Island, 57, 67, 94, 125, 139, 174
HERS Raters, 134
Home Energy Raters, 134
IES, 97, 178
Impact Categories, 183
IPMVP, 78, 79, 87, 155, 165
ISO, 66, 69, 136, 143
LEED for Homes, 133
LEED for Retails, 78, 166
LEED Rating System Selection Policy, 110, 210
LEED v4, 62, 90, 131, 132, 151, 168, 169, 171, 184, 190
Life cycle analysis, 50
Minimum Program Requirements, 132
Mnemonics, 112
MPRs, 132
Note, 228
O&M, 66

ODP, 41, 48, 52, 54, 55, 116, 121, 122, 123
Open spaces, 107
process energy, 31, 101
RECs, 50, 119
Regional Priority, 35, 105
regulated (non-process) energy, 31, 102
ROI, 43, 112
SCAQMD, 149
SCM, 149
SR, 126
SRI, 36, 41, 48, 50, 106, 116, 119, 126
stormwater, 33, 41, 48, 103, 110, 116
Tips, 217, 218, 219, 231
vegetated roof, 33, 58, 125, 126
Water Metering, 72, 94, 147, 174
weighting process, 184
Zero Emission Vehicles (ZEV), 39, 108

www.ingramcontent.com/pod-product-compliance
Lightning Source LLC
Chambersburg PA
CBHW071831300426
44116CB00009B/1507